Flight Briefing for Pilots
Volume 6

By the same authors

Flight Briefing for Pilots, Volume 1
(An Introductory Manual of Flying Training Complete with Air
Instruction)

Flight Briefing for Pilots, Volume 2
(An Advanced Manual of Flying Training Complete with Air
Instruction)

Flight Briefing for Pilots, Volume 3
(Radio Aids to Air Navigation)

Flight Briefing for Pilots, Volume 4
(Associated Ground Subjects)

Flight Briefing for Pilots, Volume 5
(Emergency Procedures for Pilots)

Flying the VOR

A Guide to Aircraft Ownership

The Tiger Moth Story

Captains and Kings

Radio Navigation for Pilots

The Instrument Rating (N. H. Birch)

Principles of Flight (Audio-visual trainer by A. E. Bramson)

Flight Briefing for Pilots

Volume 6

Examination questions and answers, complete with full index to other 5 volumes in Flight Briefing series.

N.H. Birch MSc, MRAeS
Director Hamilton-Birch Limited
Liveryman of the Guild of Air Pilots and
Air Navigators

A.E. Bramson MRAeS
Chairman of the Panel of Examiners
Liveryman of the Guild of Air Pilots and
Air Navigators

SECOND EDITION

PITMAN

PITMAN HOUSE LIMITED
39 Parker Street, London WC2B 5PB

Associated Companies
Pitman Publishing New Zealand Ltd, Wellington
Pitman Publishing Pty Ltd, Melbourne

First published in Great Britain as *Check Pilot* 1973
Reprinted 1976
Second Edition 1980

ISBN: 0273 01409 9

Text set in IBM Press Roman by Composer Typesetting, Bath
Printed and bound in Great Britain by The Pitman Press, Bath.

reface

ne of the problems of learning to fly is that most light aircraft
re noisy, expensive and anything but ideal classrooms. It is there-
ore in the interest of the pilot under training that he should not
end costly time in the air learning what is better understood
n the ground – at little or no expense. Although a classroom
ay be the ideal environment in which to learn the various ground
bjects it is by no means the only one. Not all flying schools
nd clubs provide ground school facilities and often the pilot
nder training can spare only limited time at the airfield. That
eing so, today's classroom can range from the comfort of the
ome to the commuter train. As such *Volume 6* is intended to
e your personal examiner. It is suitable for individual or group
udy.

Some of the questions may appear obvious, others rather less
, while a number will require great care. However, they are all
ased upon the depth of knowledge required for a Private Pilot's
icence and some of the higher or additional qualifications.

The questions are divided between background knowledge
nd practical application and are presented in a style similar to
at used by international aviation authorities, the 'multiple-
hoice' technique. As such they are a form of programmed learn-
g. In giving the correct answers our aim has been to provide the
eader with a little more than a simple 'right' or 'wrong' because
e believe that an incorrect answer points to a lack of under-
tanding, not only of the question but possibly the entire subject.
f you select an incorrect answer we tell you why it is wrong and
lthough to this extent *Volume 6* is a self-contained pilot
xaminer, we have taken this a stage further by quoting text

from the other volumes of *Flight Briefing for Pilots* which should clarify any misunderstandings. We hope that all pilots, student or qualified, who read this book will find it useful, informative, and dare we suggest, entertaining?

NHB
AEB

Contents

How to use this book

Any self-marking system must present even the most honest
examinee with certain temptations; the tendency to guess when the
correct answer is not known and the urge to see the next answer
while checking the one just completed. To obtain full benefit from
this book, it is suggested that the answers chosen should be listed o
paper and only checked at the back of the book when a subject ha
been completed. To discourage guessing, allow one mark for a
correct answer and minus one for those that are incorrect. 70%
constitutes a minimum pass, 80% a good pass, 90% very good and
above 90% excellent.

   Flight Briefing for Pilots has been reprinted many times since
the series was first published and it has therefore been necessary to
refer recommended reading to the most recent editions. The year o
publication and the edition number to which the page references in
this book refer, are as follows:

Volume 1 (Fourth Edition) — 1978
Volume 2 (Fifth Edition)   — 1978
Volume 3 (Fourth Edition) — 1979
Volume 4 (Third Edition)   — 1979
Volume 5 (Second Edition) — 1980

Questions
1 Navigation

1 A line drawn on a topographical map represents:
   a) A rhumb line,
   b) A great circle,
   c) An isogonal

2 When measuring required track on a topographical map the protractor should be aligned on a meridian:
   a) Near the beginning of the track,
   b) Near the destination,
   c) Near the centre of the track.

3 A track drawn on a Mercator's projection is particularly suitable for:
   a) Radio navigation,
   b) Flight over the Poles,
   c) Long distance navigation.

4 One inch on a 1:500,000 scale map represents:
   a) Approximately 4 st. m.,
   b) Approximately 8 st. m.,
   c) Approximately 8 n. m.

5 Magnetic variation is:
   a) The difference between True and Compass Heading,
   b) The difference between Magnetic and Compass Heading,
   c) The difference between True and Magnetic Heading.

6   When converting a True Heading to a Magnetic Heading
     variation is applied by:
     a)   Adding easterly and subtracting westerly variation,
     b)   Adding westerly and subtracting easterly variation,
     c)   Adding westerly and subtracting easterly variation in the
           Northern hemisphere and reversing the process south of
           the Equator.

7   The Required Track is 325°, variation 8°W, deviation 2°E and
     calculated drift 8°P. What will be the Compass Heading?
     a)   339°(C),
     b)   323°(C),
     c)   327°(C).

8   After 40 n. m. the aircraft is over a lake 4 n. m. to port of a
     track which measures 120 n. m. How many degrees, port or
     starboard, must the pilot alter heading to fly directly to the
     destination?
     a)   9°P,
     b)   9°S,
     c)   12°S.

9   After ten minutes flying you are over a bridge 25 n. m. down a
     track measuring 225 n. m. but 3 n. m. to the right. What alter-
     ation in heading will be necessary to regain track in ten
     minutes?
     a)   14°P,
     b)   8°P,
     c)   14°S.

10   There are six methods of depicting height above and depth
     below mean sea level on topographical and other maps and
     charts. Can you name them?

11   What is an isogonal?
     a)   A broken line surrounding controlled airspace,
     b)   A line on the compass correction card plotting deviation,
     c)   A line on a map or chart, usually broken, joining places
           of equal magnetic variation.

12   On a map variation may be shown by the following methods:
  a)   A correction on each meridian and a statement in words,
  b)   Isogonals, diagram, statement in words, compass rose,
  c)   A statement in words accompanied by a corrector box, a
        conversion table in the left margin and Air Information
        Circulars issued from time to time.

13   On the current 1:500,000 series of maps what is the meaning
      of this sign ⊗?
  a)   A glider site,
  b)   A naval airfield,
  c)   A disused airfield which may be unfit for use.

14   On the current 1:500,000 series of maps what is the meaning
      of this sign ▲?
  a)   A compulsory reporting point,
  b)   A non-compulsory reporting point,
  c)   An unlighted obstruction.

15   While flying over France your track runs across a spot height
      marked as 600 metres amsl. Assuming you wish to clear the
      position by 1500 ft at what altitude should you fly?
  a)   Approximately 3500 ft,
  b)   Approximately 2100 ft,
  c)   Approximately 3950 ft.

16   You plan to fly from Coventry to overhead the White Horse at
      Marlborough, then return to Coventry. On the outward flight
      you are steering 205°(M) to maintain the track of 188°(T).
      The variation is 8°W. What will be the Heading for the return
      flight?
  a)   351°(M),
  b)   007°(M),
  c)   035°(M).

17   The difference between TMG and track required is called:
  a)   Wind effect,
  b)   Drift,
  c)   Track error.

18   To assist in estimating TMG in the early stages of a map
       reading exercise the pilot should employ:

    a)   Five or ten degree fan lines drawn from the point of
            departure either side of track,

    b)   Time marks,

    c)   Ten-minute marks along track.

19   When lost a pilot should draw a circle of uncertainty on the
       map and look for features within that area. The circle should
       be:

    a)   Equal in diameter to the estimated distance flown since
            first uncertain of position,

    b)   Centred on the DR position using as radius 10% of the
            estimated distance flown since the last pinpoint
            recognized with certainty,

    c)   Centred on the DR position using as radius 10% of the
            total distance for the flight.

20   You are flying to a weekend golf meeting. The aircraft is
       unable to take the golf clubs and your suitcases in the baggage
       compartment. You should:

    a)   Tie the suitcases in the baggage compartment and lay the
            golf clubs lengthwise along the cabin,

    b)   Secure the golf clubs in an upright position between the
            front and rear seats and put the suitcases in the rear
            baggage compartment,

    c)   Place the golf clubs in the rear baggage compartment with
            as much luggage as is permitted and position the
            remaining suitcase(s) within the cabin.

21   What preparations can be made before or during flight to assist
       in revising the ETA?

    a)   Divide the track into four equal parts, time the third
            quarter and revise the ETA when starting the last quarter,

    b)   Obtain a revised W/V over the radio,

    c)   Work out distance flown every ten minutes, using
            computed ground speed and place marks along the track
            to represent ten minutes flying.

When compiling a flight plan gross errors, e.g. setting the wind or variation in the opposite direction are best avoided by:

a)   Having the flight plan checked by another pilot,

b)   Forming the habit of estimating track, drift, distance and time of flight before using the computer,

c)   Using a Mercator's Chart.

A Navigational Computer should be used for the following questions

Calculate Magnetic heading from the following data: Track req. 255°; W/V 105/15 kt; TAS 140 kt; variation 8°W.

a)   266°(M),

b)   244°(M),

c)   260°(M).

You are planning a flight from Biggin Hill to Leicester East, a distance of 100 st. m. Track required is 333° and the W/V is 290/20 kt. At a TAS of 110 MPH the aircraft is known to have a fuel consumption of 5 gal/hr. Allowing 0.6 gal for the take-off and climb how much fuel will be required for the flight?

a)   6 gal,

b)   5 gal,

c)   8 gal.

Convert 120 km to nautical miles.

a)   75 n. m.,

b)   65 n. m.,

c)   80 n. m.

Your IAS is 140 kt and the correction card for that speed reads +1 kt. The aircraft is at an altitude of 8000 ft where the OAT is +5°C. What is your TAS?

a)   124 kt,

b)   160 kt,

c)   157 kt.

27   Your TMG is 045°(T) and the G/S is 135 kt. The aircraft is o
      a Compass Heading of 045°, deviation 2°W; variation 8°W, a
      the TAS is 140 kt. What is the wind velocity?

      a)   128/25 kt,
      b)   142/22 kt,
      c)   322/25 kt.

28   Your TAS is 180 kt, the W/V is 160/20 kt and track 150°(T)
      What is the True Heading and ground speed?

      a)   151° and 160 kt,
      b)   151° and 200 kt,
      c)   178° and 131 kt.

29   You are flying at an indicated altitude of 10,000 ft. The OAT
      is −10°C. What is your true altitude?

      a)   10,200 ft,
      b)   10,550 ft,
      c)   9800 ft.

30   You are flying a light twin-engine aircraft with a fuel capacity
      of 100 gal. The journey is over a distance of 725 n. m., the
      aircraft uses 16 gal/hr while cruising at a TAS of 165 kt. On
      the flight there is an average headwind component of 20 kt.
      Allowing an additional 5 gal for the take-off and climb how
      long will the aircraft be able to hold over the destination
      allowing no reserves of fuel and assuming that the same powe
      setting is used? And how far could you divert in that time?

      a)   56 min = 135 n. m.,
      b)   2 hr   = 370 n. m.,
      c)   75 min = 181 n. m.

31   Your owners manual quotes the fuel capacity of the aircraft a
      50 U.S. gal. How much fuel in Imperial gallons will it hold?

      a)   21.6 Imp. gal,
      b)   41.6 Imp. gal,
      c)   60   Imp. gal.

2   On a day when the QNH is 1013 mb you are cleared to cruise
at flight level 75. You plan to climb at a speed of 110 kt when
the rate of climb will be 875 ft/min and at flight level 75 your
TAS is 135 kt. How long will it take to arrive over the
destination which is 108 n. m. away, assuming a 15 kt tailwind
component?

a)   40½ min,
b)   42½ min,
c)   44   min.

3   Your aircraft is refuelled at an airfield in Spain and you sign
for 136 litres. Convert this to Imperial gallons.

a)   30   Imp. gal,
b)   37½ Imp. gal,
c)   22   Imp. gal.

4   The maximum authorized weight for the aircraft is 3600 lb.
You require 50 gal for the flight. With crew and passengers but
without fuel the aircraft weighs 3080 lb. How much payload
remains for baggage allowing 7.2 lb/gal?

a)   120 lb,
b)   160 lb,
c)   360 lb.

2 Meteorology

1   **Lapse rate is temperature change with height. It changes at a rate of:**
    a) $2°F$ per 1000 ft.,
    b)   Is dependent on the humidity of the air mass,
    c) $2°C$ per 1000 ft.

2   **What is the meaning of the term dew point?**
    a)   The humidity in a frontal air mass,
    b)   The temperature at which further cooling will cause condensation,
    c)   The point at which the air ceases to rise on reaching a similar environmental temperature.

3   **When air rises there is a drop in temperature due to expansion which together with the lapse rate gives a total lapse rate which is known as:**
    a)   Adiabatic lapse rate,
    b)   Dry adiabatic lapse rate,
    c)   Saturated adiabatic lapse rate.

4   **The dry adiabatic lapse rate is:**
    a)   A temperature drop of $2°C$ per 1000 ft.,
    b)   A temperature drop of $3°C$ per 1000 ft.,
    c)   A temperature drop of $2°F$ per 1000 ft.

5   **Cirrostratus is:**
    a)   A high-level thin, veil-like cloud,
    b)   Low-level thin cloud cover in which icing is often present,
    c)   A high-level shapeless wispy cloud formation.

6   Thunder and severe turbulence is associated with:
    a)   Cumulonimbus clouds,
    b)   Nimbostratus clouds,
    c)   Altocumulus clouds.

7   A wind is said to veer when there is:
    a)   A clockwise change in direction,
    b)   A reversal in wind direction,
    c)   An anti-clockwise change in direction.

8   The earth's surface has this effect on lower winds:
    a)   It produces smoother flying conditions,
    b)   It causes a reduction in wind speed, possibly with
         turbulence,
    c)   It affects the wind speed but not its direction.

9   Radiation fog may form at night under the following
    conditions:
    a)   Clear sky with a normal adiabatic lapse rate and a moist
         air mass,
    b)   Clear sky, a gentle wind and a moist air mass,
    c)   Moist air mass, reasonable cloud cover and a dew point
         that is easily reached.

10 At ground level the circulation of wind around a depression in
    the Northern Hemisphere is:
    a)   Clockwise blowing into the centre at approximately 30°
         to the isobars,
    b)   Anti-clockwise blowing parallel to the isobars,
    c)   Anti-clockwise blowing into the centre at approximately
         30° to the isobars.

11 Airframe icing will only occur:
    a)   In cloud below freezing level,
    b)   In cloud at any ambient temperature,
    c)   In any weather conditions below freezing temperature.

12 Airframe icing will affect:
    a)   Effectiveness of controls, stalling speed and airspeed,
    b)   Effectiveness of controls, airspeed but not stalling speed,
    c)   Will decrease the stalling speed and increase the weight.

13   When flying in cloud at an outside air temperature of + 6°C:
   a)   Airframe icing may be expected,
   b)   Carburettor icing may occur,
   c)   There is no risk of airframe or carburettor icing.

14   An aircraft has been left out overnight. It is covered with an icy film which is known as:
   a)   Hoar frost,
   b)   Glazed ice,
   c)   Rime ice.

15   Flight within a cumulonimbus cloud may entail:
   a)   Moderate icing with some precipitation,
   b)   Severe turbulence, icing, lightning and hail,
   c)   Little turbulence, no precipitation but a risk of lightning strike.

16   There is an easterly wind blowing across a range of hills lying North and South. A pilot flying over is likely to notice down draughts on:
   a)   The windward side,
   b)   The leeward side,
   c)   On both the windward and leeward sides.

17   The standard barometric pressure is:
   a)   1002.3 mb.,
   b)   1003.2 mb.
   c)   1013.2 mb.

18   After landing an altimeter set on the QFE will always read:
   a)   Height above sea level,
   b)   Zero,
   c)   Airfield elevation above msl.

19   The QNH is related to:
   a)   Altitude,
   b)   Height,
   c)   Flight level.

20 When an aircraft reaches transition altitude the pilot should change his altimeter setting to:
a) QFE,
b) QNH,
c) The standard setting.

21 Buys Ballot's Law states that in the Northern Hemisphere if you stand with your back to the wind the area of lower pressure is:
a) On the right,
b) On the left,
c) Ahead.

22 A change in pressure of 1 mb will alter the reading of an altimeter by:
a) 30 ft,
b) 60 ft,
c) 90 ft.

23 When a large anti-cyclone persists during summer in the British Isles the weather during the day is likely to be:
a) Fine,
b) Low cloud with rain,
c) Thunderstorms.

24 When large cumulus clouds develop which type of precipitation may be expected?
a) Drizzle,
b) Heavy showers,
c) Hail.

25 Poor weather conditions exist but a cold front is forecast to move across the area. When the front has gone through the weather will:
a) Improve,
b) Deteriorate,
c) Remain much the same that day.

26   An aircraft is experiencing starboard drift while flying in the
      Northern Hemisphere. This indicates that:
      a)   The wind is increasing,
      b)   The aircraft is flying towards an area of low pressure,
      c)   The aircraft is flying towards an area of high pressure.

27   Dull weather with continuous drizzle prevails but a warm front
      is expected to pass through and afterwards flying conditions
      will:
      a)   Be much improved,
      b)   Include some drizzle and poor visibility,
      c)   Include a risk of thunderstorms.

28   When flying in turbulence it is important to:
      a)   Increase the airspeed,
      b)   Decrease the airspeed,
      c)   Use 10° of flap to lower the stalling speed.

29   The lines joining positions of equal pressure on a synoptic
      chart are called:
      a)   Isobars,
      b)   Contour lines,
      c)   Millibars.

30   An occluded front is:
      a)   A poorly developed inactive cold front,
      b)   A combination of a cold and warm front,
      c)   A poorly developed warm front.

31   The wind was 270/20 kt, which of the following has veered?
      a)   240/20 kt,
      b)   300/20 kt,
      c)   270/10 kt.

32   Advection fog is caused by:
      a)   Industrial smoke mixing with moist air,
      b)   A moist air mass being lifted over high ground,
      c)   A moist air mass drifting over a colder surface.

33   The station model is found:

    a)   On a Synoptic Chart,

    b)   In a meteorological forecast,

    c)   On a route forecast.

34   What are super-cooled water droplets?

    a)   Water droplets that form into snow while falling through cloud,

    b)   Water droplets that remain in the liquid state at below freezing temperature and which freeze on impact with a surface,

    c)   Water droplets that cause rime ice.

35   A series of closely-spaced isobars on a weather map indicates:

    a)   High winds,

    b)   Low winds,

    c)   Possibility of a temperature inversion.

3 Aviation Law

1   The holder of a Commercial Pilot's Licence may fly for hire
    and reward:
    a)   Single-engine aircraft of any weight,
    b)   Singles or multis of any weight,
    c)   Aircraft, singles or multi-engine, not exceeding 12,500 lbs
         (5,700 kg) MATO weight.

2   A Private Pilot's licence is valid for:
    a)   One year,
    b)   Three years,
    c)   Permanently.

3   An aircraft in group 'B' is:
    a)   A single-engine aircraft above 12,500 lb MATO weight,
    b)   A single-engine aircraft below 12,500 lb MATO weight,
    c)   A multi-engine aircraft below 12,500 lb MATO weight.

4   The holder of a Private Pilot's Licence may:
    a)   Fly passengers for hire and reward, only within the UK,
    b)   Fly passengers anywhere in the world but not for hire
         and reward,
    c)   Fly passengers for hire and reward outside the UK.

5   In order to maintain a group on a Pilot's Licence without
    having to take a flight test the holder must have flown an
    appropriate aircraft within the previous 13 months for not less
    than:
    a)   5 hr,
    b)   10 hr,
    c)   10 hr of which 5 hr may be in a simulator.

6   To obtain a night rating a pilot with the required day flying
     experience must complete at least:
     a)   5 hr instrument instruction and 5 hr night flying under
           supervision,
     b)   5 hr instrument instruction and 10 hr night flying under
           supervision,
     c)   10 hr instrument instruction and 5 hr night flying under
           supervision.

7   When two aircraft are approaching head on:
     a)   Each aircraft shall alter heading to the left,
     b)   The smaller aircraft shall alter heading to the right,
     c)   Each aircraft shall alter heading to the right.

8   When two aircraft are flying on converging headings:
     a)   The one which has the other on its port side shall give
           way,
     b)   Both shall turn onto diverging headings,
     c)   The one which has the other on its starboard side shall
           give way.

9   When two aircraft are approaching to land at the same time:
     a)   The one which has the greater height must give way to
           the lower aircraft,
     b)   The larger aircraft has right of way,
     c)   The one nearest the runway threshold has right of way to
           land.

10   Above 3000 ft outside controlled airspace a pilot must fly
     within the following weather conditions to remain VMC:
     a)   1 mile horizontally and 1000 ft vertically from cloud and
           3 n. m. visibility,
     b)   1 mile horizontally and 1000 ft vertically from cloud and
           5 n. m. visibility,
     c)   1 mile horizontally and 500 ft vertically from cloud and
           5 n. m. visibility.

11   In the UK flight at night under VFR:
     a)   Is not permitted,
     b)   May be permitted,
     c)   Is permitted only when the pilot has an instrument
           rating.

12   An area where firing and bombing practice is permanently active by day and night is indicated on a map by:
   a)   A pecked or dotted red outline,
   b)   A solid blue outline,
   c)   A solid red outline.

13   Using the quadrantal rule a pilot making good a magnetic track of 180° would fly:
   a)   Odd thousands of feet + 500 ft,
   b)   Even thousands of feet + 500 ft,
   c)   Even thousands of feet.

14   When flying under VFR, flight separation is the responsibility of:
   a)   ATC in the Flight Information Region,
   b)   The pilot,
   c)   ATC Service on the frequency being worked.

15   Other than during a landing or take-off, normally an aircraft may not fly close to persons or property. This limit is:
   a)   500 ft,   b)   1000 ft,   c)   2000 ft.

16   For flights abroad certain aircraft documents are required. These must include:
   a)   C of A, General Declaration, Certificate of Maintenance,
   b)   General Declaration, Fuel Carnet, C of A,
   c)   C of A, Radio Installation Licence, General Declaration.

17   Two red balls on the signals mast coupled with a double cross in the signals area denotes:
   a)   Parachute dropping is in progress,
   b)   Instrument meteorological conditions in force,
   c)   Glider flying is in progress.

18   An intermittent white beam directed to an aircraft on the ground indicates:
   a)   Expedite take-off,
   b)   Return to the parking area,
   c)   Flight plan has been cancelled.

19   A pilot may file a flight plan at any time but it is mandatory:
   a)   If it is intended to fly over the sea,
   b)   If radio is not installed in the aircraft,
   c)   For flight at night.

20   The UK is divided into the following flight information regions:
   a)   London and Scottish,
   b)   London, Midland and Scottish,
   c)   Southern, Preston and Northern.

21   Following the malfunction of the undercarriage or flaps an R/T call should be prefixed by the words:
   a)   Mayday-Mayday-Mayday,
   b)   Security-Security-Security,
   c)   Pan-Pan-Pan

22   At night a military airfield may be identified by a beacon flashing in morse:
   a)   The airfield letters in green,
   b)   The airfield letters in red,
   c)   The airfield letters in white and red.

23   When using a prominent line feature for navigational purposes the pilot should:
   a)   Fly to the right of the feature,
   b)   Fly overhead the feature,
   c)   Fly to the left of the feature.

24   Flying instruction for the purpose of gaining a licence or rating may be given by:
   a)   Any pilot with a professional licence,
   b)   A qualified flying instructor,
   c)   Any licenced pilot so long as no payment is made.

25   Shortly before a night landing the radio fails and visual signals have to be used. The pilot sees a steady red beam directed at him from the ground. This means:
   a)   Land at another airfield,
   b)   Return to your point of take-off,
   c)   Landing temporarily suspended; wait.

26   In the UK transition altitude for civil airfields is:

    a)   4000 ft amsl,

    b)   3000 ft amsl,

    c)   3000 ft amsl, with certain exceptions, e.g. the London, Manchester and Scottish TMAs, where it is 6000 ft amsl.

27   While flying at night you see the green navigation light of another aircraft flying on a similar heading at the same height as your aircraft. It appears to be coming closer. What action would you take?

    a)   Hold the present height and heading but be ready to take avoiding action if this is required.

    b)   Alter heading to starboard,

    c)   Climb.

28   The UK Board of Trade Accident Investigation Department must be notified when an accident involves:

    a)   A forced landing due to engine failure,

    b)   Damage in a hangar during maintenance,

    c)   Damage due to a technical defect in the aircraft.

29   While taxying back to the parking area you see a vehicle towing an aircraft moving towards your intended path. What action should you take?

    a)   Proceed on your present direction since you have right of way,

    b)   Turn right,

    c)   Take such avoiding action as is appropriate. The towing vehicle has right of way.

30   A detailed explanation of UK aviation law is given in:

    a)   The Air Navigation Order and Rules of the Air and ATC Regulations,

    b)   The General Aviation Flight Guide,

    c)   Aeronautical Information Circulars.

4 Principles of Flight

1 **When air is induced to flow over an airfoil section:**
   a) Pressure is reduced over the top surface,
   b) Pressure is increased over the top surface,
   c) Pressure is reduced over the top surface and increased below the lower surface.

2 **The centre of pressure is:**
   a) The point through which the total effect of lift may be said to act,
   b) The point at which maximum drag occurs,
   c) The force opposing the centre of gravity.

3 **The angle of attack is:**
   a) The angle between the airfoil chord line and the relative airflow,
   b) The angle between the relative airflow and the angle of incidence of the wing,
   c) A constant determined by the manufacturers.

4 **For a given airspeed lift increases:**
   a) As the angle of attack is increased,
   b) As the centre of pressure moves forward,
   c) As the angle of attack increases and the centre of pressure remains constant.

5 **As the angle of attack is increased:**
   a) The drag is reduced,
   b) The drag remains the same if the speed is unchanged,
   c) The drag is increased.

6   While performing its stabilizing function the tailplane:
    a)   Produces no lift,
    b)   Produces lift,
    c)   Produces a correcting force, either up or down.

7   Directional stability achieved by the fin is also influenced by:
    a)   The keel surface or area behind the centre of gravity,
    b)   Movement of the centre of pressure,
    c)   Using the 'high wing' design.

8   If the profile drag at 100 kt were found to be 200 lb, the drag at 200 kt would be:
    a)   400 lb,
    b)   800 lb,
    c)   1200 lb.

9   The primary effect of aileron is to cause movement in the rolling plane. The further or secondary effect is:
    a)   Yaw followed by a spiral dive,
    b)   A skid outwards,
    c)   A nose-up attitude as a result of increased lift on the up-going wing.

10   The further effect of rudder causes:
    a)   The aircraft to slip,
    b)   A movement in the rolling plane,
    c)   A movement in the rolling plane followed by a spiral dive.

11   When the elevator trim tab is set in the up position this will:
    a)   Assist the pilot to maintain a nose-up attitude
    b)   Will slow down the airflow over the control surface and make it more effective,
    c)   Assist the pilot to maintain a nose-down attitude.

12 When an aircraft is flying straight and level at a constant IAS the forces are as follows:
  a) Lift and weight are equal and drag is proportional to the relative airflow,
  b) Lift and weight are equal and thrust is proportional to the relative airflow,
  c) Lift and weight components are equal and thrust is equal to drag.

13 When power is adjusted in level flight the slipstream will tend to affect:
  a) The longitudinal stability,
  b) Directional stability,
  c) Lateral stability.

14 The maximum rate of climb is achieved at:
  a) A low airspeed and a high power setting,
  b) A high airspeed and a high power setting,
  c) A compromise between speed and power setting.

15 Flaps are fitted to an aircraft for the purpose of:
  a) Increasing lift and drag while decreasing the stalling speed,
  b) Increasing drag, increasing payload and increasing the stalling angle,
  c) Increasing lift, drag and stalling speed.

16 In addition to the usual benefits, a Fowler flap:
  a) Provides a pre-stall buffet,
  b) Increases the wing area,
  c) May be used to improve the take-off.

17 In a correctly executed rate 1 turn an aircraft will change direction at:
  a) $360°$ per min,
  b) $2°$ per sec,
  c) $3°$ per sec.

18   During a turn total lift balances weight and:
   a)   Accelerates the aircraft towards the centre of the turn,
   b)   Balances weight and does not affect the turn,
   c)   Has no turning force, the increased lift resulting from the
         outer wing travelling faster than the inner wing during the
         turn.

19   The rate of turn is dependent on:
   a)   The airspeed and the angle of bank,
   b)   The airspeed and the angle of attack,
   c)   The angle of bank and the power available.

20   Which of these statements is correct?
   a)   Stalling can only occur in certain attitudes,
   b)   Stalling can occur in almost any attitudes,
   c)   Stalling can only occur when the airspeed is low.

21   The anti-servo tab on an all-flying tailplane:
   a)   Moves in the same direction as the main surface to assist
         the pilot by removing control loads,
   b)   Moves in the opposite direction to the main surface to
         assist the pilot by removing control loads,
   c)   Moves in the same direction as the main surface to assist
         the pilot by adding control loads.

22   During a spin an aircraft is simultaneously:
   a)   Pitching up, yawing and rolling,
   b)   Pitching down, yawing and turning,
   c)   Pitching up and down, yawing to the accompaniment of
         severe slip towards the spin axis.

23   To recover from a spin the aircraft must be made to:
   a)   Stop rolling with aileron and attain level flight with
         power and elevator.
   b)   Stop the roll with opposite rudder and attain level flight
         with power and elevator,
   c)   Stop yawing with opposite rudder, decrease its angle of
         attack with forward elevator, keep straight after spinning
         stops and then resume level flight with correct attitude
         and power.

24   There are four possible causes of swing during a take-off.
      Those affecting a nosewheel aircraft are:
      a)   Torque effect and slipstream effect,
      b)   Slipstream effect, gyroscopic effect and torque effect,
      c)   Asymmetric blade effect, and torque effect.

25   During a short take-off, use of the recommended flap setting
      will:
      a)   Decrease the take-off run and increase the rate of climb,
      b)   Decrease the take-off run, increase the climb angle and
            probably reduce the rate of climb,
      c)   Decrease the take-off run without affecting the rate of
            climb.

26   In a turn at a steep angle of bank:
      a)   The stalling speed is increased because the angle of attack
            must be increased,
      b)   The stalling speed is increased because the wing loading is
            increased,
      c)   The stalling speed is increased because of the inclined lift.

27   Mass balance is fitted to some controls for the purpose of:
      a)   Assisting the pilot to move a heavy control surface,
      b)   Preventing flutter,
      c)   Opposing aerodynamic loads during high 'g' manoeuvres.

28   Lateral stability is built into an aircraft by incorporating the
      following features:
      a)   High wing, dihedral angle, sweepback, high keel surface,
      b)   Dihedral angle, wash-out, Frise ailerons,
      c)   Dihedral angle, wash-out and slats.

29   Some control surfaces are fitted with horn balance for the
      purpose of:
      a)   Preventing flutter,
      b)   Preventing aileron drag,
      c)   Relieving the pilot of otherwise heavy control loads.

30   On some aircraft small strips are fixed to the leading edges of
the wings, close to the fuselage. Their purpose is to:
   a)   Make the aircraft stall more cleanly,
   b)   Prevent a wing dropping at the stall,
   c)   Prevent a wing dropping at the stall and provide a pre-
stall warning in the form of a buffet.

31   When a wing drops during stalling practice the ailerons must
not be used to regain lateral level because:
   a)   The down-going aileron on the wing to be raised would
be more fully stalled causing an increase in drag and the
risk of a spin,
   b)   At low speeds near the stall the ailerons are not very
effective,
   c)   The up-going aileron on the wing to be raised would
aggravate the situation.

32   It is potentially dangerous to commence a gliding turn at a low
airspeed because:
   a)   The risk of stalling is greater in a turn,
   b)   At low speeds there is a risk of aileron reversal,
   c)   There is a risk of an incipient spin developing.

33   A wing is most efficient when it is flown at an angle of attack
of $3\frac{1}{2}°-4°$. This is called:
   a)   The riggers angle of incidence,
   b)   Minimum drag angle,
   c)   Best lift/drag angle.

34   Most aircraft have a tailplane. What is its purpose?
   a)   To provide longitudinal stability,
   b)   To carry the elevators,
   c)   To cater for changes in weight and balance.

35   What is wheelbarrowing?
   a)   The tendency to pitch forward during landing due to
harsh application of the brakes,
   b)   The tendency during take-off or landing for the aircraft
to run along on the nosewheel with the main undercarriage off the ground,
   c)   Instability on the ground due to a faulty nosewheel
steering damper.

5 Engines and Propellers

1   **Too weak a fuel/air mixture in a piston engine will cause:**
    a)   High fuel consumption and black smoke from the exhaust,
    b)   Loss of fuel pressure,
    c)   Loss of power, overheating and possibly detonation.

2   **Movement of the pilot's throttle control alters:**
    a)   The main jet,
    b)   The butterfly valve,
    c)   The power jet.

3   **Operation of the idle cut-off stops the engine by:**
    a)   Cutting off fuel supply to the slow running jet,
    b)   Cutting off fuel supply to the carburettor float chamber,
    c)   Earthing the ignition.

4   **With most aero engines in popular use each cylinder provides a power stroke:**
    a)   Every two engine revolutions,
    b)   Every four engine revolutions,
    c)   Every engine revolution.

5   **In a piston engine, in-going mixture and out-going burned gases are controlled by:**
    a)   The carburettor heat control,
    b)   The mixture control,
    c)   The inlet and exhaust valves.

6   Two separate ignition systems are fitted to an aero engine for the purpose of:
a)   Safety in the event of an ignition failure,
b)   To provide better combustion and safety in the event of an ignition failure,
c)   To assist engine starting.

7   When the ignition is switched 'off' the magnetos are prevented from generating sparks because:
a)   The magnetos are earthed to the engine,
b)   The battery has been switched off,
c)   The plug leads have been disconnected from the magnetos.

8   When the tanks are in the mainplane of a low-wing design fuel starvation in the event of a failed mechanical fuel pump is safeguarded by:
a)   Gravity feed,
b)   The throttle-operated accelerator pump,
c)   An electric fuel pump.

9   Carburettor icing is of three types:
a)   Fuel evaporation, impact and throttle ice caused by adiabatic cooling,
b)   Rime, hoar frost and glazed ice,
c)   Fuel evaporation, rime and glazed ice.

10   The development of carburettor icing may be recognized by:
a)   A gradual decrease in RPM, rough running and eventually complete loss of power,
b)   Severe misfiring and fluctuation of the rpm indicator,
c)   Sudden loss of power.

11   Before the first flight of the day it is good practice to check the ignition is off, then turn over the engine by hand before starting. Why?
a)   To fill the cylinders with mixture and make the engine ready for a cold start,
b)   To break the oil film adhesion and so reduce the load on the starter, to check the cylinder compressions and to check for hydraulicing,
c)   To prime the oil system.

12   Assuming little or no wind and no met or air traffic
      restrictions a pilot wishing to fly for maximum range must
      adopt the following procedure:
      a)   Select a low altitude and fly at the minimum power
            setting for level flight,
      b)   Fly at a high altitude in weak mixture and at the
            minimum power setting for level flight,
      c)   Climb to an altitude where full throttle is required to
            maintain an indicated best L/D speed and weaken the
            mixture.

13   During take-off nosewheel aircraft have less tendency to swing
      than tailwheel types because:
      a)   There is no gyroscopic or asymmetric blade effect from
            the propeller and nosewheel undercarriages have good
            directional stability,
      b)   The pilot has a better view ahead,
      c)   Slipstream effect cancels torque effect.

14   When the power setting is altered there is a tendency to yaw
      due to:
      a)   Offset fin or fixed rudder trim,
      b)   Gyroscopic effect,
      c)   Slipstream and torque effect.

15   When an aircraft is fitted with a fixed-pitch propeller a change
      in airspeed will alter the engine RPM. Why is this?
      a)   Because of asymmetric blade effect,
      b)   Because an increase in airspeed will remove some of the
            load from the propeller and allow an increase in RPM
            while a decrease in airspeed has the reverse effect,
      c)   Because changes in airspeed alter the amount of air
            passing through the induction system and this affects
            engine power.

16   If a coarse-pitch propeller (fixed) ensures a high cruising speed
      why are they not always fitted to light aircraft?
      a)   Because of noise limitations,
      b)   To avoid high fuel consumption,
      c)   Because a poor take-off performance results from this
            type of propeller.

The following questions relate to constant-speed propellers and multi-engine aircraft

17   **The purpose of fitting a constant-speed propeller is to:**
   a)   Improve the cruise performance,
   b)   Provide the most efficient blade angle for all phases of flight,
   c)   Improve take-off performance.

18   **Why do some propellers have three or more blades instead of just two?**
   a)   To absorb high engine powers without resorting to propellers of very large diameter,
   b)   To provide safety in the event of a blade failure,
   c)   To increase the airflow over the wing and tail surfaces.

19   **The lowest speed at which a light twin-engine aircraft will maintain direction when an engine fails during take-off is:**
   a) V_1 (decision speed),
   b) V_2 (safety speed),
   c) V_{mca} (minimum control speed, air).

20   **While turning to the left the starboard engine fails. The aircraft will then:**
   a)   Roll out of the turn,
   b)   Steepen its angle of bank,
   c)   Yaw to the right and roll to the left.

21   **During asymmetric flight a turn is commenced at a low air-speed. Full rudder proves unable to keep the balance indicator in the centre. The pilot should:**
   a)   Reduce power on the live engine,
   b)   Move the control wheel forward and increase air-speed,
   c)   Reduce the angle of bank.

22   **During the cruise an engine fails without warning or evidence of serious trouble. The pilot should:**
   a)   Feather immediately,
   b)   Try to find the cause of failure and re-start the engine before considering feather action,
   c)   Take immediate engine fire action.

23 While flying on instruments an engine fails. The turn and slip indicator will show:

    a) A yaw towards the dead engine with a skid in the opposite direction,

    b) A yaw towards the live engine with a skid in the same direction,

    c) A yaw towards the live engine with a skid in the opposite direction.

24 The ability to feather the propeller when an engine fails confers these advantages on a multi-engine aircraft:

    a) Reduction of asymmetric drag and the prevention of further damage to the engine.

    b) A shorter landing run.

    c) Fuel for the dead engine may be transferred to the live engine.

25 What is the meaning of the term 'zero thrust'?

    a) A power setting used to simulate a feathered engine for the purpose of safe asymmetric training,

    b) The power setting achieved at full throttle altitude,

    c) A power setting which produces neither thrust nor drag during a descent.

26 A high outside air temperature has this effect on the engine-out performance of a twin-engine aircraft:

    a) A decrease in single-engine TAS,

    b) A decrease in single-engine ceiling,

    c) An increase in V_2 (safety speed).

27 Some engines are fitted with a fuel injection unit in place of a carburettor. What is the reason for this?

    a) To prevent condensation in the fuel system,

    b) To increase the power of the engine,

    c) To improve fuel economy and reduce the risk of engine icing.

28   During cruising flight it is noticed that changes of airspeed are accompanied by corresponding alterations in engine RPM on one engine. What is the most likely fault causing this?

a)   Propeller on affected engine locked in positive fine pitch,

b)   Low oil pressure on the affected engine,

c)   Failure of the constant speed unit on the affected engine.

29   At the start of the climb-out after take-off an engine fails. With full rudder direction cannot be maintained. The pilot should:

a)   Throttle back the live engine,

b)   Maintain safety speed and assist the rudder with aileron applied in the same direction,

c)   Abandon the take-off and land ahead.

30   What is the purpose of cross feed?

a)   A feature of the fuel system designed to prevent an air lock,

b)   A feature of the fuel system used when checking for water in the tanks,

c)   A feature of the fuel system for the purpose of making all the fuel carried in the aircraft available to any engine.

6 Airframes

1 **Stressed skin aircraft are constructed as follows:**
   a) Metal sheets riveted to steel tubes,
   b) Outer sheets attached to a light structure of longerons and frames. The airframe may be of wood or metal,
   c) Pressed aluminium alloy with no supporting frame.

2 **In a modern aircraft fitted with a cantilever wing weight is supported by:**
   a) One or more spars of considerable depth,
   b) A series of ribs,
   c) Internal wire bracing.

3 **Flutter is caused by:**
   a) Turbulent airflow over the wings,
   b) Turbulent airflow over the wings and the tail surfaces,
   c) Vibration due to flexing of the ailerons, rudder and/or elevators.

4 **Some control surfaces carry a small metal tab on their trailing edge for the purpose of:**
   a) Providing trim adjustment by bending to the correct position,
   b) Indicating the manufacturer's part and release numbers,
   c) Discharging static electricity and improving radio reception.

5 **Flaps which not only depress but also increase the wing area by extending backwards on tracking are called:**
   a) Slotted flaps,
   b) Kruger flaps,
   c) Fowler flaps.

6   Undercarriage struts utilising compressed air and oil for springing and damping are known as:
   a)   Oleo struts,
   b)   Hydraulic jacks,
   c)   Pneumatic actuators.

7   Disc brakes are preferable to drum units because:
   a)   They last longer,
   b)   They do not fade to the same extent under heavy use,
   c)   They can be hydraulically operated.

8   In a light aircraft hydraulic pressure for the brakes is provided by:
   a)   Master cylinders operated by the pilot's hand or feet,
   b)   An engine driven pump,
   c)   A venturi tube.

9   Control locks are provided:
   a)   To prevent unauthorised use of the aircraft,
   b)   To protect the control surfaces while moving the aircraft in and out of the hangar,
   c)   To avoid wind damage while the aircraft is parked on the ground.

10   Some high wing monoplanes have struts running from the bottom of the fuselage to the mainplanes for the purpose of:
   a)   Providing a foothold to assist while refuelling,
   b)   Supporting the wing while the aircraft is on the ground,
   c)   Supporting the wing while the aircraft is on the ground and when it is flying.

7 Instruments

1 Blockage of the static tube or vent will affect the following
   instruments:
   a)   ASI, Altimeter and VSI,
   b)   ASI, Altimeter and Turn Indicator,
   c)   Altimeter, VSI and Turn Indicator.

2 There is an appreciable elapse of time before the ASI settles
   to a new airspeed. Why is this?
   a)   Lag in the instrument,
   b)   Inertia of the aeroplane,
   c)   Position error.

3 The difference between IAS and RAS is caused by:
   a)   Position error,
   b)   Instrument error,
   c)   Position and Instrument error.

4 A low air density due to altitude and high temperature will
   have this effect:
   a)   Give an increased TAS for any RAS,
   b)   Give a decreased TAS for any RAS,
   c)   Give a TAS that is less than RAS.

5 The altimeter obtains its pressure sample from:
   a)   The static line or static vent,
   b)   The pressure line,
   c)   A venturi tube.

6   A sensitive altimeter at low levels is accurate to within limits
     of:
     a)   + or − 20 ft,
     b)   + or − 350 ft,
     c)   +30 or − 45 ft.

7   **What is the standard ICAN Barometric pressure?**
     a)   1013 mb at mean sea level and 0°C,
     b)   1013.2 mb at mean sea level and at a temperature of
           +15°C,
     c)   1013.2 mb at mean sea level and +10°C.

8   **You are flying into an area of high pressure. The altimeter
     will:**
     a)   Under read,
     b)   Over read,
     c)   Be unaffected.

9   **For the purpose of instrument flying high rates of descent
     must be avoided because:**
     a)   The gyro instruments may topple,
     b)   The aircraft may exceed its V_{ne},
     c)   The altimeter will lag seriously under conditions of high
           rates of vertical change.

10. **You take-off from an airfield with an elevation of 150 ft amsl
     having set the Regional QNH of 1012 mb. The destination is a
     non-radio airfield situated on a 600 ft hill within the same
     altimeter setting region. What QFE setting should be used for
     the landing?**
     a)   997 mb,
     b)   992 mb,
     c)   1032 mb.

11   **For the purpose of calibrating an altimeter a temperature of
     −5°C is assumed at 10,000 ft. What effect will a lower
     temperature have on the aircraft's true height when the
     instrument reads 10,000 ft?**
     a)   It will be above 10,000 ft,
     b)   It will be below 10,000 ft,
     c)   No effect because temperature changes are compensated
           by a bi-metal link.

12   Within a temperature range of +50°C and −20°C the vertical
      speed indicator is accurate to within limits of:
      a)   ±200 ft/min,
      b)   ± 30 ft/min,
      c)   ±100 ft/min.

13   Viewed face-on a gyroscope is rotating in a clockwise
      direction. Where should you apply a force to make it twist to
      the left (i.e. the right-hand rim will move away from you)?
      a)   Against the top face of the rotating gyro,
      b)   Against the right face of the rotating gyro,
      c)   Against the right edge of the gyro, inwards towards the
            centre.

14   The following instruments on the flight panel are gyro
      operated:
      a)   Artificial horizon, direction indicator and turn and slip
            indicator,
      b)   Artificial horizon, direction indicator and turn indicator,
      c)   Artificial horizon, direction indicator and slip indicator.

15   Why do some gyro instruments topple when the aircraft is
      placed in an extreme attitude?
      a)   Because the air supply to the gyro is discontinued,
      b)   Because the Pendulous Unit is displaced beyond its
            operating range,
      c)   Because the Gimbals come up against their limiting stops.

16   Which gyro operated instrument may be relied upon to give
      factual information during the recovery from a spin (assuming
      the instruments fitted have toppling limits)?
      a)   The turn indicator,
      b)   The slip indicator,
      c)   The artificial horizon.

17   Before take-off the direction indicator must be synchronized
      with the magnetic compass. Why is this?
      a)   Because the gyro may not have reached its correct
            operating speed,
      b)   To allow for local magnetic variation,
      c)   Because a direction indicator has no means of seeking
            Magnetic North.

18   At regular intervals during flight the direction indicator must
      be re-set against the magnetic compass. Why is this?
      a)   Because of mechanical drift,
      b)   Because of mechanical drift, apparent drift and transport
            error.
      c)   Because of turbulence.

19   What feature is incorporated in the direction indicator for the
      purpose of correcting the effects of apparent drift?
      a)   A spring attached to one of the gimbals,
      b)   An adjustable drift nut attached to one of the gimbals,
      c)   A pendulous unit.

20   What is the principal advantage of a gyro-magnetic compass
      over a direction indicator?
      a)   There are no toppling limits,
      b)   It is suitable for Polar Navigation,
      c)   It incorporates its own north-seeking device and an auto-
            matic synchronizing system.

21   In a vacuum-operated artificial horizon, automatic erection of
      the gyro is performed by:
      a)   The pendulous unit,
      b)   A caging device,
      c)   A counter-weight on the horizon bar.

22   You have just taken-off in a fast aircraft fitted with a vacuum-
      operated artificial horizon. While climbing straight ahead the
      instrument will for a short while indicate:
      a)   A high nose-up attitude,
      b)   A climbing turn to the left,
      c)   A climbing turn to the right.

23   How is vacuum provided for the gyro operated instruments?

   a)   By the static tube,

   b)   By an engine-driven pump or a venturi tube,

   c)   By the static vent.

24   What is the meaning of the term 'dip' as applied to the magnetic compass?

   a)   The tendency for the magnet system to tilt during turns,

   b)   The residual deviation present after a compass swing,

   c)   The tendency for the magnet system to be pulled down towards the Earth's magnetic field.

25   In the Northern Hemisphere what effect will acceleration and deceleration have on an easterly or westerly compass reading?

   a)   An apparent turn to South and North respectively,

   b)   An apparent turn to North and South respectively,

   c)   No change.

26   While on a northerly heading within the Southern Hemisphere the aircraft is flown left wing low. What effect will this have on the compass card?

   a)   The south-seeking edge of the compass card will swing towards the lower wing,

   b)   The north-seeking edge of the compass card will swing towards the lower wing,

   c)   No change.

27   When using a magnetic compass in the Northern Hemisphere what is the correct technique for turning onto N, S, E and W?

   a)   Roll out of the turn $25°-30°$ before reaching North, $25°-30°$ after reaching South and $5°-10°$ before reaching East or West.

   b)   Roll out of the turn $25°-30°$ after reaching North, $25°-30°$ before reaching South and $5°-10°$ before reaching East or West,

   c)   Roll out of the turn $25°-30°$ before reaching North, $25°-30°$ before reaching South, $5°-10°$ before reaching East and $5°-10°$ after reaching West.

The following questions relate to the use of instruments.

28   Although the required heading is being maintained the ball of
the slip indicator is over to the left. What correction is
required to resume balanced flight?
a)   Left rudder until the ball centres,
b)   Left rudder until the ball centres together with right
aileron to level the artificial horizon,
c)   Right rudder until the ball centres together with right
aileron to level the artificial horizon.

29   While practising instrument flying you inadvertently place
yourself in a position where the instruments indicate a
balanced rate 4 turn to the left coupled with a rapid loss of
height and a rapid increase in airspeed. What is the aircraft
doing?
a)   Spinning to the left,
b)   In a spiral dive to the left,
c)   A steep turn to the left with the pressure tube blocked.

30   While climbing at full throttle on instruments you note that
although the airspeed is correct the rate of climb is considerably
below normal. What action should you take?
a)   Adopt a higher nose attitude on the artificial horizon and
re-trim,
b)   Lower the nose slightly and increase the climbing speed
by approximately 5 kt,
c)   Check for carburettor icing.

31   The artificial horizon has become unserviceable during instrument flying. The aircraft enters a steep dive with the airspeed
increasing rapidly. During the recovery what indication from
the remaining instruments will tell you when the nose is on or
near the horizon?
a)   When the ASI returns to normal cruising speed,
b)   When the ASI stops increasing and the altimeter stabilizes,
c)   At the point where the ASI stops increasing and begins to
move towards the original cruising speed.

32   What angle of bank should you adopt on the artificial horizon
     for a rate 1 turn while flying at an IAS of 130 kt?
     a)   15°,
     b)   18°,
     c)   20°.

33   While flying a twin-engine aircraft on instruments there is a
     sudden turn to the right accompanied by a loss of height and
     considerable left rudder is required to regain and hold level
     flight. What is the cause of this and how will it be confirmed
     by the other instruments?
     a)   Uneven flow of fuel from the wing tanks which will be
          confirmed by the fuel gauges,
     b)   Faulty rudder trim confirmed by the turn and slip
          indicator,
     c)   Failure of the starboard engine confirmed when its mani-
          fold pressure gauge remains at atmospheric pressure while
          the throttle is adjusted, gradual lowering of its oil and
          cylinder-head temperatures and a lower airspeed.

34   While flying a twin-engine aircraft on instruments the artificial
     horizon indicates 5° left wing low and this is confirmed by the
     turn needle. When corrected with right aileron the slip
     indicator moves out to the right. What is the cause of this?
     a)   The fixed aileron trim tab requires adjusting,
     b)   Incorrect rudder trim,
     c)   The engines are not synchronized.

35   The direction indicator has failed and it is necessary to
     continue instrument flight using the magnetic compass as the
     sole heading indicator. When making timed rate 1 turns
     through a required number of degrees a pilot should:
     a)   Allow 3° per second and start timing after the correct
          angle of bank has been attained.
     b)   Allow 3° per second. Start timing when rolling into the
          turn and roll out after the required number of seconds
          have elapsed.
     c)   Allow 3° per second. Start timing when rolling into the
          turn and aim to have the wings level again after the
          required number of seconds have elapsed.

8 Radio Aids to Air Navigation

1   A QDM is:
    a)   The magnetic bearing of an aircraft from a station,
    b)   The true bearing of an aircraft in relation to a station,
    c)   The Magnetic heading to be steered by an aircraft to reach a station in conditions of no wind.

2   A class 'A' bearing is accurate within:
    a) $\pm 1°$,
    b) $\pm 3°$,
    c) $\pm 2°$.

3   Other than VHF, radio bearings taken at night are:
    a)   Less accurate than those taken by day,
    b)   More accurate than those taken by day,
    c)   Unaffected.

4   If the Magnetic heading is $045°$ and the radio compass reads $225°$ the QDM to the beacon is:
    a) $180°$,
    b) $270°$,
    c) $225°$.

5   A pilot wishes to track out from an NDB on a heading of $220°$. Assuming no wind he will do this when:
    a)   The radio compass and DI both read $220°$,
    b)   The radio compass reads $180°$, the DI reads $220°$,
    c)   The DI reads $180°$, the radio compass reads $220°$.

6   The pilot wishes to maintain a QDM of 270° to the NDB. The
     DI indicates 270° and although the radio compass reads 000°
     this immediately commences to decrease because:
     a)   The wind is from the left,
     b)   The wind is from the right,
     c)   The pilot has overflown the beacon.

7   While joining an NDB holding pattern an aircraft turns left
     from outbound 090° onto inbound 270°. Assuming the turn is
     proceeding correctly what reading should be on the radio
     compass when the DI indicates 300°?
     a)   300°,
     b)   270°,
     c)   330°.

8   When flying a holding pattern in conditions of cross wind the
     amount of drift should be:
     a)   Trebled when flying inbound,
     b)   Trebled when flying outbound,
     c)   Allowed equally when flying inbound and outbound.

9   When an EAT of 1230 has been passed by ATC to a pilot this
     indicates that:
     a)   He is not expected to the airfield facility before that
           time,
     b)   The descent may not be commenced before that time,
     c)   The landing may not be made before 1230.

10   Having overflown the NDB the pilot turns onto an outbound
     heading of 090°. The radio compass reads 185° and this
     immediately begins to increase:
     a)   There is starboard drift,
     b)   There is port drift,
     c)   The beacon has not been correctly overflown.

11   When taking up the hold on an NDB above transition level the
     altimeter must be set to:
     a)   Regional QNH,
     b)   Airfield QNH,
     c)   1013.2 mb.

12   A pilot is completing an NDB let-down to the decision height
      when he is instructed to overshoot. He will reset his altimeter
      to:
      a)   1013.2 mb,
      b)   QFE,
      c)   QNH.

13   To maintain a QDM of 270° with 10° starboard drift the DI
      and radio compass will read:
      a)   260° and 000°,
      b)   270° and 010°,
      c)   260° and 010°.

14   An aircraft flying to an NDB is instructed to leave the beacon
      on a northerly heading. To do this the pilot overflies the NDB,
      turns onto a heading of 015° to gain the QDR and when this
      occurs the radio compass will read:
      a)   165°,
      b)   180°,
      c)   195°.

15   After tuning and identifying a VOR station it may be used for
      orientation by rotating the OBS until the deviation needle
      centres when:
      a)   QDM is read off the main scale with TO showing,
      b)   QDR is read off the main scale with TO showing,
      c)   QDM is read off the main scale with FROM showing.

16   While heading 010° towards a VOR station a W/V of 090/15
      kt causes the aircraft to drift to port. The VOR indicator
      would read:
      a)   OBS 010° TO, deviation needle LEFT,
      b)   OBS 010° FROM, deviation needle LEFT,
      c)   OBS 010° TO, deviation needle RIGHT.

17   While using VOR as a let-down aid the pilot selects 170° on
the OBS and maintains this QDM for the final approach. After
overflying the VOR station the deviation needle indications
should be:

a)   Flown in the corrective sense,

b)   Flown in the reverse sense,

c)   Ignored when so close to the station.

18   An aircraft flying on a heading of 200° crosses the 270° radial
of a VOR station. Since the OBS is set reading 090° TO the
deviation needle is central. If the aircraft continued on its
present heading what would be the next VOR indication?

a)   No change,

b)   Fly right,

c)   Fly left.

19   Full deflection of the deviation needle, left or right represents
a departure from the selected radial of approximately:

a)   2½°.

b)   10°,

c)   20°.

20   Full deflection of the deviation needle with the 'OFF' flag
showing indicates that:

a)   The VOR station is off the air,

b)   The VOR receiver has failed,

c)   The aircraft is on a radial many degrees removed from
that selected on the OBS.

21   An aircraft is homing towards a VOR station situated 80 n.m.
distant. Within how many miles, port or starboard of track
indicated may the pilot expect to be?

a)   3 n.m.,

b)   4 n.m.,

c)   2 n.m.,

22   A VOR indicator may be used when tuned to an ILS
      frequency. When used to guide an aircraft on the approach the
      OBS should be:
      a)   Ignored since it has no effect on the deviation needle,
      b)   Set to the runway QDM,
      c)   Set to zero.

23   While homing to an airfield a pilot receives successive QDMs of
      $010°$, $000°$ and $357°$. This indicates that:
      a)   The wind is from the left,
      b)   The wind is from the right,
      c)   The station has been overflown.

24   At a distance of 3 n. m. from touchdown a pilot on a
      Surveillance Radar Approach should be passing through the
      following height:
      a)   1100 ft,
      b)   950 ft,
      c)   800 ft.

25   A radar approach is normally terminated:
      a)   At the runway threshold,
      b)   ½ mile or 2 miles from the threshold, depending on
            procedure,
      c)   At the airfield OCL.

26   The vertical needle on the ILS indicator relates to:
      a)   The glide path,
      b)   The localizer,
      c)   Is interrelated to glide path and localizer.

27   When flying the QDR of the runway, indications of the ILS
      localizer needle are:
      a)   In the corrective sense (i.e. needle left-fly left),
      b)   Inoperative,
      c)   In the reverse sense.

28   When established on the localizer and approaching the ILS
      glide path the glide path needle will:
      a)   Give a maximum 'fly up' signal,
      b)   Give a maximum 'fly down' signal,
      c)   Remain central until the glide path is intercepted.

29   The ILS outer marker is indicated by:
   a)   A flashing amber light,
   b)   A flashing white light,
   c)   A flashing blue light.

30   An aircraft is above the glide path and to the right of the
     runway centre line. ILS indications would be:
   a)   Glide path needle DOWN — Localizer needle LEFT,
   b)   Glide path needle UP — Localizer needle LEFT,
   c)   Glide path needle UP — Localizer needle RIGHT.

31   An aircraft is below the glide path and to the left of runway
     centre line. ILS indications would be:
   a)   Glide path needle UP — Localizer needle RIGHT,
   b)   Glide path needle DOWN — Localizer needle LEFT,
   c)   Glide path needle UP — Localizer needle LEFT.

32   When filing an airways flight plan flight levels are:
   a)   In accordance with the quadrantal rule,
   b)   Related to the direction of the airway,
   c)   Varied according to the traffic density.

33   What is a fan marker?
   a)   A position indicator used in conjunction with Loran,
   b)   A VHF beacon transmitting a continuous signal which
        may be monitored on the airborne radar,
   c)   An airways marker beacon operating on a frequency of
        75 MHz which triggers a coded identification signal that
        may be heard through a headset or identified on the
        white marker light.

34   When flying over the facility at a height of 12,000 ft agl the
     DME indicator will read:
   a)   2 n. m.,
   b)   Zero,
   c)   OFF.

35   At low levels VHF transmissions are of limited range. This is
      because:
      a)   The equipment is of low power,
      b)   There is no ground wave,
      c)   There is no sky wave and the ground wave is interrupted
            by solid objects including the surface of the Earth.

9 Airfield Performance, Weight and Balance

1 **The highest weight at which an aircraft may take off is known as:**
   a) Maximum Authorised Take-off Weight,
   b) Maximum Ramp Weight,
   c) Certified Take-off Weight.

2 **The Owner's/Operating/Flight Manual for larger aircraft usually quotes Zero Fuel Weight. What does this mean?**
   a) The legal minimum fuel that may be carried for any flight,
   b) The maximum weight authorised exclusive of fuel,
   c) The maximum weight authorised inclusive of fuel.

3 **The Useful Load of an aircraft may be determined by:**
   a) Subtracting Empty Weight and weight of fuel from Maximum Authorised Take-off Weight,
   b) Subtracting the maximum weight of fuel from Gross Weight,
   c) Subtracting the Equipped Empty Weight from Maximum Authorised Take-off Weight.

4 **It is particularly dangerous to load an aircraft so that its C of G is aft of limits because:**
   a) There is an increase in stability and the controls have less effect,
   b) A tail-heavy aircraft is a potential spinning risk and stability is degraded,
   c) Too much weight is concentrated on the mainwheels of the undercarriage.

5   Centre of Gravity limits in the aircraft are quoted in the Owner's/Operating/Flight Manual in the following form:
   a)   A total weight,
   b)   A number of pound-inches of Kg-mm,
   c)   Two figures in inches or mm measured in relation to a particular datum point.

6   A beam is balanced at its centre and a 200 kg weight is then positioned 3 metres from the pivot point. To restore balance what weight must be placed at a distance of one metre on the other side of the pivot?
   a)   600 kg,
   b)   600 kg less half the weight of the beam,
   c)   66.66 kg.

7   A Loading Graph is used:
   a)   To calculate airfield take-off performance against aircraft weight,
   b)   As a simple means of calculating moments for each passenger, baggage and fuel station,
   c)   To ensure that the correct proportion of fuel and payload is loaded into the aircraft.

8   A Load Sheet is used:
   a)   To calculate total weight of the aircraft,
   b)   To calculate total moment,
   c)   To calculate total weight and total moment.

9   An aircraft that normally lifts off at 70 kt takes off with a 7 kt tailwind. This will:
   a)   Reduce the rate of climb,
   b)   Reduce the take-off run by 20%,
   c)   Increase the take-off run by 20%.

10   An aircraft that is taking-off from a 'hot and high' airfield will:
   a)   Need a longer run than usual,
   b)   Need a shorter run than usual,
   c)   Take the same run as usual but lift off at a higher than average indicated airspeed.

11   **Flaps should be used for take-off:**
   a)   On all occasions,
   b)   To improve the rate of climb,
   c)   Only when recommended in the Owner's/Operating/
         Flight Manual.

12   **Additional to the usual considerations that apply to single-engine designs, the danger of overloading a multi-engine aircraft is that there is:**
   a)   A risk of straining the undercarriage,
   b)   A serious reduction (or complete elimination) of engine-
         out rate of climb and a general deterioration in engine-out
         performance,
   c)   A reduction in stability due to adverse B/A Ratio.

Answers
1 Navigation

Answer		Comments and Study References
1	b)	A Rhumb Line crosses all meridians at the same angle and an Isogonal is a line joining all places of equal magnetic variation. If you answered (a) or (c) read MAPS AND CHARTS, p. 187 of Vol. 1, also AERONAUTICAL MAPS AND CHARTS on p. 145 of Vol. 4.
2	c)	Maximum error would occur when measuring track at either end. Remember, the meridians converge towards the Poles. If you answered (a) or (b) read MEASURING TRACK on p. 189 of Vol. 1, and study Fig. 90.
3	c)	Radio bearings are always Great Circles (shortest distance between two points on a spherical surface). Since lines drawn on a Mercator's Chart are not Great Circles they are therefore not ideal for radio navigation. If you answered (a) or (b) read the paragraph at the top of p. 190, Vol. 1.
4	b)	The 1:250,000 scale represents approximately 4 statute miles to the inch. If you answered (a) or (c) read SCALE on p. 190 of Vol. 1.
5	c)	To convert a True Heading into a Compass Heading two corrections are required, one — local magnetic variation and two — deviation caused by the aircraft itself. If you answered (a) or (b) read VARIATION on p. 107 and DEVIATION on p. 109 of Vol. 4.
6	b)	Remember the little couplet — 'East is least and West is best.' This holds true North and

South of the Equator. If you answered (a) or (c) read
ALLOWING FOR VARIATION AND DEVIATION on
p. 110 of Vol. 4.

7 a) If you said 323° (C) drift was applied in the wrong
direction and in the case of answer (c) variation and
deviation were applied in the incorrect sense. Think
about it.

8 b) If the aircraft is to port of track the alteration must be in
the opposite direction. Read **THE ONE IN SIXTY
RULE**, p. 202 Vol. 1, and the explanation starting at the
bottom of p. 141 of Vol. 4.

9 a) 8° port would take you directly to the destination but
the question asked for a correction to regain track in ten
minutes, the time already flown. In this case the distance
to run is irrelevant. If you answered (b) or (c) read **THE
1-IN-60 RULE**, bottom of p. 141 until '. . . to his
destination, B' on p. 142 of Vol. 4 and study Fig. 65.

10   1. Spot Heights (and depths),
     2. Layer Tints,
     3. Contours,
     4. Form Lines,
     5. Hill Shading,
     6. Hachures. If you were unable to remember them read
     RELIEF, top of p. 192, Vol. 1 and the detailed explan-
     ations that follow.

11 c) The line surrounding controlled airspace is simply a
boundary. If you answered (a) or (b) read **VARIATION**
on p. 107 to the top of p. 109 in Vol. 4.

12 b) Meridians cannot be corrected for magnetic variation
otherwise it would be impossible to use them for
determining position. A corrector box is fitted to a
magnetic compass for the purpose of eliminating
deviation, the tables in the left margin of most maps are
for the purpose of converting feet to metres and Air
Information Circulars are not used for promulgating

Variation. If you answered (a) or (c) read items (a), (b), (c) and (d) immediately above DEVIATION on p. 109, Vol. 4.

13   c)   There is no separate symbol for Naval airfields. If you got this wrong study an up-to-date 1:500,000 map or look at the symbols shown in Fig. 69, p. 149 of Vol. 4.

14   a)   If you answered (b) or (c) study an up-to-date 1:500,000 map or look at the symbols shown in Fig. 69 (cont) on p. 150 of Vol. 4.

15   a)   The first step is to convert 600 metres to feet and there is a table printed in the left margin of the 1:500,000 series maps for the purpose. Alternatively you could have used the circular slide rule on a navigational computer. The method shown on p. 137 of Vol. 4 (CONVERTING STATUTE MILES, NAUTICAL MILES AND KILO-METRES) and Fig. 62 are relevant except that for this problem the '60' mark on the inner scale should be set against the 'KILO/KM-M-LTR' mark on the outer scale and the answer read against the mark 'FEET'. In this problem the '60' mark represents 600 metres.

16   b)   The first step must be to determine drift and this is only possible when True Track is compared with True Heading, or Magnetic Track is compared with Magnetic Heading. Answer (a) is the result of finding drift by using True Track and Magnetic Heading while in answer (c) the correct drift has been found and doubled for the return flight, then applied in the wrong direction. If you got this wrong read MAKING GOOD A RECIPROCAL TRACK on p. 145 of Vol. 4 and study Fig. 68.

17   c)   Wind effect is the difference between Hdg/TAS and TMG/Ground Speed while Drift is the angle between Heading and TMG. The correct answer forms the basis of the '1-in-60' rule. This is an important tool of Pilot Navigation and if you answered (a) or (b) read THE 1-IN-60 RULE, bottom of p. 141 in Vol. 4. The term Track Error appears on the following page.

18   a)   Time Marks or Ten Minute Marks are different names for
the same thing and they are used as an aid to anticipating
pinpoints. If you answered (b) or (c) read from 'Within
the first five or ten minutes . . . ' in the centre of p. 201
to the end of that section on p. 202 of Vol. 1 and study
Fig. 96.

19   b)   When lost the error will have occurred after the last pin-
point was recognized with certainty. If you answered (a)
or (c) read ACTION TO BE TAKEN WHEN LOST on
p. 207 of Vol. 1.

20   c)   Modern golf clubs have steel shafts and they must be kept
well away from the magnetic compass. If you answered
(a) or (b) read DEVIATION on p. 109 of Vol. 4.

21   a)   A revised W/V would involve handling the computer
while flying and working out a new Heading and Ground
Speed using a wind that is in any case only estimated.
Ten Minute Marks may be an aid to map reading but they
are of little assistance in revising the ETA. If you
answered (b) or (c) read TIME on p. 204 of Vol. 1.

22   b)   Unless he is experienced the other pilot may be a less
proficient navigator than you and a Mercator's Chart is
usually unsuited for pilot navigation. If you answered (a)
or (c) read the first four paragraphs of THE FLIGHT
PLAN on p. 204 and 206 of Vol. 1.

23   c)   An answer like 266° (M) would indicate that you have
applied the wind in the opposite direction while (b) is a
case of Variation applied in the wrong sense. If you
selected (a) or (b) read HOW TO FIND Hdg(T) and G/S
(and DRIFT) on p. 127 of Vol. 4, study Figs. 57 and 58
– and don't forget, 'East is least and West is best'
(ALLOWING FOR VARIATION AND DEVIATION,
p. 110, Vol. 4).

24   a)   Here is a case where the aircraft's speed is quoted in
MPH (no doubt because the ASI is calibrated that way)
so it is therefore more convenient to measure distances in
statute miles. This means converting the wind speed from

20 kt to 23 MPH, giving a G/S of 92 MPH and an elapse time of 65 min. If you made an error on the computer read CALCULATING TIME AND DISTANCE ON FUEL REMAINING, p. 137 of Vol. 4.

25   b)   If you said 75, that is the answer in statute miles while answer (c) means you have set 120 against 'WEIGHT IN KILOGRAMMES' instead of the 'KILO/KM-M-LTR' on the outer scale of the computer. Read CONVERTING STATUTE MILES, NAUTICAL MILES AND KILOMETRES on p. 137 of Vol. 4 and study Fig. 62.

26   b)   Answer (a) will occur if you use the outer scale for RAS and the inner scale to find TAS. The two scales should in fact be used the other way round. You will arrive at answer (c) if $-5°C$ is set on the computer instead of $+5°C$. If you got this wrong read AIRSPEED INDICATOR AND ALTIMETER CORRECTIONS, on p. 139 of Vol. 4, and study Fig. 63.

27   c)   Answer (a) is the result of applying Variation and Deviation incorrectly. 'East is least and West is best' only applies when converting from True to Magnetic and from Magnetic to Compass. Here is a case where we know the Compass Heading and must convert to True so the $2°W$ and $8°W$ must be applied in the opposite sense. If you got this wrong read HOW TO FIND W/V WHEN Tr. AND G/S ARE KNOWN on p. 129 of Vol. 4, and study Figs. 59 and 60.

28   a)   Answer (b) will result when the wind is applied in the reverse direction and (c) is the product of two errors; using the TAS as Track and the Track as TAS. If you answered (b) or (c) read HOW TO FIND Hdg(T) AND G/S (AND DRIFT) on p. 127 of Vol. 4, and study Figs. 57 and 58.

29   c)   (a) is the result of reading from the outer to the inner scale on the circular slide rule while (b) is the answer that will occur with an OAT of $+10°C$ whereas the question said that the temperature was $-10°C$. If you chose (a) or

(b) read ALTIMETER CORRECTIONS on p. 141 of
Vol. 4.

30   a)   This is a simple matter of converting time at 16 gal/hr
into total gallons used, after allowing an extra 5 gal for
the take-off and climb. If you answered (b) or (c) read
CALCULATING TIME AND DISTANCE ON FUEL
REMAINING on p. 137 of Vol. 4.

31   b)   If you align 50 against the 'U.S. GAL' mark on the outer
scale of the computer the answer may be read against the
'IMP GAL' position.

32   c)   Here is a problem embracing slight variations on some of
the previous exercises and calling for a little common
sense. The first step should be to jot down the Ground
Speed in the climb and in the cruise, in this case 125 kt
and 150 kt respectively, allowing for the 15 kt tailwind.
Next determine the proportion of the flight at each
speed. This is decided for you by the time required to
reach Flight Level 75 (on this day corresponding to an
altitude of 7500 ft). To find time of climb set 1 (actually
10) on the inner scale against 875 on the outer scale.
Look for 75 (your flight level) on the inner scale and read
off 8½ min for the climb. The remainder of the problem
is a simple matter of time and distance. An 8½ min climb
at 125 kt will cover a distance of 17.6 n. m. leaving 90.4
n. m. to complete the journey which at 150 kt means
another 35½ min.

33   a)   This is a straightforward conversion using the relevant
marks on the computer's outer edge, i.e. 'KILO/KM-M-
LTR' for the litres to be converted and 'IMP GAL' for
the answer.

34   b)   To find the weight of 50 gal at 7.2 lb/gal, set 1 (actually
10) on the inner scale against 7.2 on the outer scale, then
find the weight against 50 on the inner scale which is
360 lb. Add this weight of fuel to the 3080 lb, subtract
from the maximum authorized weight of 3600 lb and the
result is the weight available for baggage.

2 Meteorology

Answer		Comments and Study References
1	c)	These days the °F scale is rarely used in aviation. If you answered (a) or (b) read TEMPERATURE on p. 67 of Vol. 4.
2	b)	An understanding of the meaning of DEW POINT is important because this is the starting point of all fog and cloud formations. If you answered (a) or (c) read HUMIDITY AND AIR MASSES on page 68 of Vol. 4.
3	b)	It is only after the Dew Point has been reached and cloud has begun to form that the air is saturated with moisture. If you answered (a) or (c) read TEMPERATURE on p. 67 to the top of p. 68 in Vol. 4.
4	b)	Answer (a) is the lapse rate with height without the influence of further cooling due to expanding, rising air. If you answered (a) or (c) read the first five lines at the top of p. 68 in Vol. 4.
5	a)	Any cloud name beginning with 'Cirrus' or 'Cirro' is high while 'Stratus' (at any level) denotes a layer formation. If you answered (b) or (c) study CLOUDS (on p. 69 to the top of p. 70 in Vol. 4) and look at the cloud photographs mentioned in that section.
6	a)	The deciding factor in this question is the word thunder and that can only mean one type of cloud. If you answered (b) or (c) read CUMULONIMBUS on p. 70 of Vol. 4.

7   a)   If you have difficulty in remembering whether 'veer' means clockwise or anti-clockwise there can be no mistaking the direction of the opposite term 'back' since this is the same as putting the clock back or anti-clockwise. If you answered (b) or (c) read VEERING AND BACKING on p. 70 of Vol. 4.

8   b)   While much will depend upon the nature of the ground even a smooth surface is bound to retard the wind, perhaps cause eddies and therefore turbulent flying conditions. This is explained under SURFACE WINDS on p. 71 of Vol. 4. Answer (c) is also incorrect because a reduction in wind speed due to ground friction alters the balance of the Geostropic wind. Read from 'On a weather map . . . ' p. 76 to ' . . . Geostrophic wind (Fig. 29)' on p. 78 of Vol. 4, also study Figs. 28 and 29.

9   b)   Fog is not caused by ascending air therefore adiabatic cooling is not involved and answer (a) is incorrect. Cloud cover would have the effect of retaining heat below its base and so prevent the drop in temperature required for radiation fog. If you answered (a) or (c) read RADIATION FOG on pp. 71 and 73 of Vol. 4.

10   c)   This is another case of having to remember which is clockwise and which anti-clockwise. Those who have difficulty may care to remember 'we may have a low aunty but at least we have a high clock'. Answer (b) would be correct for winds at 1500 ft and higher. This is explained on p. 76 of Vol. 4 ('On a weather map . . . ' to ' . . . Geostrophic wind (Fig. 29 on p. 78)'.

11   c)   One of the mistaken beliefs of aviation is that airframe icing will only occur in cloud. If you answered (a) or (b) read ICE ACCRETION on p. 91 to ' . . . a change in flight level' on p. 92 in Vol. 4.

12   a)   A decreased stalling speed as a result of increased weight is an aerodynamic contradiction (read FACTORS AFFECTING THE STALL, item (a) on p. 94 of Vol. 1). If you answered (b) or (c) read PRINCIPAL CAUSE OF GLAZED ICE on p. 92 of Vol. 4.

13   b)   Airframe icing will not occur at a temperature of +6°C.
          While no pilot in this day and age should be in doubt
          about this question if you did answer (a) or (c) **as a
          matter of urgency** read CARBURETTOR ICING on p. 40
          of Vol. 2 and CARBURETTOR HEAT CONTROL on
          p. 26 of Vol. 4.

14   c)   This is a case of understanding how the various types of
          airframe ice are formed. If you answered (a) or (b) read
          ICE ACCRETION on p. 91 to top of p. 95 in Vol. 4.

15   b)   Clouds of considerable vertical extent are always associ-
          ated with turbulence and the developed cumulus or
          cumulonimbus represents an extreme case. Therefore
          answer (c) must be incorrect while (a) makes no mention
          of turbulence or the likelihood of hail. Read THUNDER-
          STORMS on p. 97 of Vol. 4.

16   b)   If you answered (a) or (c) read from 'The behaviour of
          wind . . .' on p. 96 of Vol. 4 to ' . . . conditions of strong
          wind' at the top of p. 97 and study Fig. 40.

17   c)   If you answered (a) or (b) 'no comment' but read THE
          ALTIMETER, on pp. 99—100 of Vol. 4.

18   b)   If you answered (a) or (c) read ALTIMETER SETTINGS
          on pp. 100—102 of Vol. 4.

19   a)   If you answered (b) or (c) read ALTIMETER SETTINGS
          on pp. 100—102.

20   c)   If you answered (a) or (b) read STANDARD ALTI-
          METER SETTING on p. 100 of Vol. 4.

21   b)   If you can remember that answer (c) is wrong it is then a
          matter of deciding if the area of low pressure is to the left
          or right. To help you decide read HORIZONTAL
          PRESSURE CHANGES AND THE ALTIMETER, page
          103 of Vol. 4 to the end of that section on p. 105 and
          study Fig. 44.

22   a)   If you answered (b) or (c) read the starting paragraph on
          p. 105 of Vol. 4.

23 a) Other than a tendency for haze generally a high-pressure system is always associated with good weather (see ANTI-CYCLONE OR HIGH on p. 78 of Vol. 4).

24 b) The larger the rain drop the more vertically developed will be the cloud of origin and this rules out answer (a). Hail is more usually associated with cumulonimbus clouds. If you answered (a) or (c) read PRECIPITATION on p. 74 of Vol. 4.

25 a) Unless there is another depression moving in behind the cold front its passing must bring a period of much improved weather. This is best understood by studying the two-dimension illustration (Fig. 34) on p. 85 of Vol. 4.

26 b) To answer this question Buys Ballot's Law must be understood. This is explained in the section headed HORIZONTAL PRESSURE CHANGES AND THE ALTIMETER, page 103 to p. 105. Also study Fig. 44 on p. 104.

27 b) The passing of a warm front heralds the Warm Sector. If you are not clear about flying conditions within this part of a low-pressure system read THE WARM FRONT bottom of p. 82 of Vol. 4. Also study Fig. 34 on p. 85.

28 b) Increasing the airspeed while flying in turbulent conditions can only add to the strains imposed on the airframe while lowering flap without reducing IAS below the Flap Limiting Speed could likewise cause airframe damage. If you answered (a) or (c) read from 'To reduce the risk of structural damage . . . ' middle of p. 95 to the end of paragraph (b) in Vol. 4.

29 a) Contour lines are used to illustrate shape on maps and charts. If you answered (b) or (c) read the third paragraph commencing 'On a weather map . . . ' on p. 76 of Vol. 4.

30 b) If you answered (a) or (c) read the second paragraph on p. 84 of Vol. 4 and study Fig. 35.

31   b)   If you answered (a) or (c) read VEERING AND
          BACKING on p. 70 of Vol. 4.

32   c)   Smoke mixing with moist air results in what the popular
          press call 'smog' or industrial haze. A moist air mass that
          is cooled through being lifted over high ground causes
          Orographic Cloud, not fog. If you answered (a) or (b)
          read ADVECTION FOG on p. 73 of Vol. 4.

33   a)   While the Station Model is used by a meteorologist to
          draw a Synoptic Chart on which to base his forecasts it is
          not part of a pilot's route or other forecast. If you
          answered (b) or (c) read from 'The position of each
          reporting station . . . ' on p. 87 of Vol. 4 to the end of
          that section and study Fig. 36.

34   b)   Water droplets that form into snow are unlikely to
          present the pilot with any hazard whereas super-cooled
          water droplets often will. If you answered (a) or (c) read
          PRINCIPAL CAUSE OF GLAZED ICE on p. 92 of Vol.
          4. Also study Fig. 38.

35   a)   Isobars that are closely spaced may be regarded as
          contour lines. On a map closely spaced contour lines
          denote a steep rise (or fall) in surface level. Likewise
          closely spaced isobars on a weather map indicate a steep
          fall or rise in pressure. If you answered (b) or (c) read the
          third paragraph commencing 'on a weather map . . . ' on
          p. 76 of Vol. 4 .

3 Aviation Law

1   c)   If you answered (a) or (b) read the last sentence of COMMERCIAL PILOTS' LICENCES, which appears on p. 173 of Vol. 4.

2   c)   Private Pilot's Licences are permanent, although medical certificates must be renewed at intervals, which may be every year or two years, according to the pilot's age.

3   c)   If you answered (a) or (b) see the first paragraph on p. 172 of Vol. 4.

4   b)   If you answered (a) or (c) read the sentence above the heading COMMERCIAL PILOTS' LICENCE on p. 172 of Vol. 4.

5   a)   If you answered (b) or (c) read from 'In order to maintain . . . ' on p. 172 of Vol. 4 to the end of that paragraph.

6   a)   If you answered (b) or (c) read NIGHT RATING, bottom of p. 175 in Vol. 4.

7   c)   Answer (b) would be impossible in practice. How could one tell if a similar aircraft was larger or smaller from a distance of perhaps several miles? If you answered (a) or (b) read No. 3 under RIGHT OF WAY IN THE AIR on p. 180, Vol. 4 and study Fig. 71.

8   c)   If you answered (a) or (b) read No. 2 under RIGHT OF WAY IN THE AIR on p. 180, Vol. 4 and study Fig. 70.

9   a)   If you answered (b) or (c) read No. 7 RIGHT OF WAY
            IN THE AIR p. 180 in Vol. 4.

10   b)   The question relates to flights above 3000 ft. The rule
            allows pilots to remain VMC over the top of cloud. If you
            answered (a) or (c) read RELATED WEATHER
            CONDITIONS No. 1, p. 182 in Vol. 4.

11   b)   In the UK all night flying is classed as IFR and this is
            mentioned under 2 (iii) on p. 183 of Vol. 4. The
            following proviso (iv) on that page explains that pilots
            without an instrument rating may obtain a Special VFR
            Clearance, conditions permitting.

12   c)   If you answered (a) or (b) read RESTRICTED AREAS
            on p. 190 of Vol. 4.

13   c)   Since the Quadrantal Rule may often be the only means
            of ensuring separation from other aircraft while flying in
            marginal weather outside controlled airspace it is vital
            that the procedure should be fully understood. If you
            answered (a) or (b) **as a matter of urgency** read FLIGHTS
            OUTSIDE CONTROLLED AIRSPACE AND THE
            QUADRANTAL RULE, pp. 191–192 and study Fig. 77
            in Vol. 4. The Quadrantal Rule extends from 3000 ft to
            25,000 ft when the high-level semi-circular rules apply.
            This is explained at the bottom of p. 192 and top of
            p. 193.

14   b)   In-flight separation is a responsibility that is shared
            between pilots and the Air Traffic Control Service. The
            dividing line is contingent upon the type of flight plan
            and the weather. This aspect of aviation law touches on
            one of the foundation stones of safety in the air. If you
            answered (a) or (c) read AIR TRAFFIC CONTROL on
            p. 182 of Vol. 4, also 2(i) under RELATED WEATHER
            CONDITIONS on the following page.

15   a)   If you answered (b) or (c) read LOW FLYING pp. 193–
            194 of Vol. 4.

16   c)   When flying abroad the Certificate of Maintenance is, perhaps surprisingly, not required. While a Fuel Carnet is very useful it is not a legal document. If you answered (a) or (b) read FLIGHTS ABROAD on p. 201 of Vol. 4.

17   c)   While most aircraft these days have good radio, ground signals are still important. If you answered (a) or (b) study the ground signals illustrated in Appendix 2 of Vol. 4.

18   b)   Like the previous question, light signals may appear irrelevant in these days of good radio communications but even the best equipment has been known to fail. Then the ability to recognize light and other signals could do much to ease an otherwise difficult situation. If you answered (a) or (c) read VISUAL SIGNALS on pp. 196–197 of Vol. 4.

19   c)   While for most non-airways flights a pilot is not required to file a flight plan he should nevertheless book out. This is in his own interest. If you answered (a) or (b) read THE FLIGHT PLAN on p. 200 of Vol. 4.

20   a)   Answer (b) is the name of a now defunct railway company and (c) is also incorrect. If you made the wrong selection read CONTROLLED AIRSPACE at the bottom of p. 183 to middle of p. 184 in Vol. 4 and study Fig. 74.

21   c)   If you answered (a) or (b) read EMERGENCY on p. 161 of Vol. 4.

22   b)   If you answered (a) or (c) read BEACONS on p. 196 of Vol. 4.

23   a)   If you fly overhead the feature it will most likely remain out of view and alternative (c) would present a hazard to pilots who knew the answer to this question and obeyed the rule. This is explained under No. 5 of RIGHT OF WAY IN THE AIR, p. 180 of Vol. 4. (Also see Fig. 73.)

24   b)   No instruction given to a student by any non-qualified instructor pilot, whatever his experience, is admissible for the purpose of gaining a licence or rating, even when no payment is involved. If you answered (a) or (c) read FLYING INSTRUCTOR'S RATING on p. 177 of Vol. 4.

25   c)   If you answered (a) or (b) read VISUAL SIGNALS on
            pp. 196–197 in Vol. 4.

26   c)   If you answered (a) or (b) read TRANSITION
            ALTITUDE on p. 20 of Vol. 3.

27   a)   This is a case where another aircraft is converging with its
            starboard wingtip on your port side (the position of air-
            craft navigation lights is explained on p. 195 of Vol. 4.
            Also see Fig. 78). While No. 2 under RIGHTS OF WAY
            IN THE AIR p. 180, Vol. 4 shows that the other aircraft
            must alter heading this does not absolve you from taking
            evasive action should this prove necessary.

28   c)   If you answered (a) or (b) read AIRCRAFT ACCIDENTS
            on p. 198 of Vol. 4.

29   c)   An aircraft being towed by a vehicle is an unwieldy com-
            bination and must surely warrant every consideration. If
            you answered (a) or (b) read RIGHT OF WAY ON THE
            GROUND, 3, on p. 180 of Vol. 4.

30   a)   While much information, mainly of an operational and
            facility nature is contained in The General Aviation
            Flight Guide, the fountain head is that mentioned in
            answer (a). If you selected (b) or (c) read from 'The fore-
            going information . . . ' on p. 201 of Vol. 4 to the end of
            the chapter.

4 Principles of Flight

Answer		Comments and Study References

1   c)   Answer (a) is only part of the story and if (b) were true aeroplanes would always remain firmly on the ground. If you answered (a) or (b) read the first three paragraphs under BEHAVIOUR OF AN AIRFOIL SECTION, p. 3 of Vol. 1 and study Figs. 5 and 6.

2   a)   The Centre of Pressure refers to Lift, therefore answer (b) is incorrect. Since it is not a force but the point through which total lift is exerted, (c) is also incorrect. If you chose either answer read from 'Lift is generated . . . ', centre of p. 6 to CENTRE OF PRESSURE in Vol. 1, also study Figs. 9 and 10.

3   a)   The Angle of Incidence is measured between the fuselage datum line and the airfoil chord line. While this is fixed by the manufacturer, Angle of Attack is under the control of the pilot. If you answered (b) or (c) read the whole of BEHAVIOUR OF AN AIRFOIL SECTION (p. 3 to the end of that section p. 10 of Vol. 1) and study the diagrams referred to in the text.

4   a)   Forward movement of the Centre of Pressure is a by-product of increased lift, not its cause. For this reason answers (b) and (c) are incorrect and if you selected either of these read No. 1, ANGLE OF ATTACK top of p. 10 of Vol. 1 and study Fig. 12.

5   c)   If drag reduced as we increased the angle of attack the IAS would increase as the stick was moved back. Answer (b) is also incorrect because you cannot increase the angle of attack and have the airspeed remain unchanged. If you

answered (a) or (b) read from 'unfortunately while
producing life. . . ' on p. 6 of Vol. 1 to ' . . . usually
occurs at 3½°–4° (Fig. 12)' on p. 8 and study Fig. 12.

6   c)   If you answered (a) or (b) read THE AEROPLANE,
p. 11 of Vol. 1 to ' . . . function of the tailplane clear'
on p. 14 and study all the diagrams mentioned in the
text.

7   a)   Movement of the Centre of Pressure in fact causes
longitudinal instability while the 'high wing' layout is
sometimes used to create lateral stability. If you
answered (b) or (c) read the paragraph commencing
'Notwithstanding the addition . . .', bottom of p. 14 in
Vol. 1 and study Fig. 21.

8   b)   Aerodynamic forces vary according to the square of the
speed (V^2 law). If you answered (a) or (c) read PROFILE
DRAG, pp. 1–2 of Vol. 2.

9   a)   If you answered (b) or (c) read FURTHER EFFECTS OF
AILERON on p. 35 of Vol. 1 and study Fig. 30.

10   c)   If you answered (a) or (b) read FURTHER EFFECTS OF
RUDDER on p. 37 of Vol. 1 and study Fig. 31.

11   c)   When the trim tab moves UP it displaces the elevator
DOWN and this in turn will raise the tail and lower the
nose. If you answered (a) perhaps you were a little
confused, while answer (b) indicates a serious lack of
knowledge on this particular subject. In either case read
THE TRIMMING CONTROLS, p. 38, Vol. 1 to '. . . the
stick' p. 39 and study Fig. 33.

12   c)   All aerodynamic forces – not just drag – are proportional to the relative airflow and thrust is proportional
to the power output of the engine. If you answered (a) or
(b) read page 51 to '. . . the aircraft will descend' top of
p. 52 in Vol. 1 and study Fig. 35.

13   b)   While to a minor extent power changes will affect longitudinal and lateral stability the main disturbance is
directional. If you answered (a) or (c) read from 'Changes

in throttle . . . ' on p. 52 of Vol. 1 to ' . . . the best arrangement' on p. 53 also study Fig. 36.

14 a) A high airspeed must reduce the rate of climb. Answer (c) is incorrect because maximum power is required for maximum rate of climb. If you answered (b) or (c) read from p. 58 to the top of p. 60 in Vol. 1 and study Fig. 38.

15 a) Slats, not Flaps, increase the stalling angle of the basic airfoil and Flaps do not increase the stalling speed as suggested in answer (c). Read THE LANDING APPROACH, pp. 65–67 in Vol. 1.

16 b) Flaps are not fitted to provide a pre-stall buffet and Fowler Flaps are not unique in offering improved take-off performance when the correct technique is used. However they are unusual in improving lifting power partly by increasing the wing area. This is shown in Fig. 42, p. 66 of Vol. 1.

17 c) If you answered (a) or (b) read from 'the number of degrees . . . ' (bottom of p. 75) to ' . . . illustrated in Fig. 48' on p. 76 in Vol. 1 and study Fig. 47.

18 a) While it is true that extra lift is produced by the outer (faster) wing during a turn the effect of this is a tendency to overbank. If you answered (b) or (c) read from p. 74 of Vol. 1 to ' . . . than that desired' on p. 75 and study Fig. 46.

19 a) Angle of attack affects airspeed and power available is the factor limiting the steepness of the turn. If you answered (b) or (c) read from 'Rate of turn . . . ' on p. 76 of Vol. 1 to the end of that paragraph.

20 b) Other than in a steep dive stalling can occur in any attitude and a 'g' manoeuvre capable of considerably increasing the wing loading could cause a stall at almost any speed within the range of the aircraft. If you answered (a) or (c) read FACTORS AFFECTING THE STALL on p. 94 of Vol. 1 and the previous paragraph beginning 'stalling can occur . . . ' on p. 93. Also study Fig. 59.

21   c)   A Balance Tab moves in the opposite direction to the
main control (see BALANCE TABS on p. 18 of Vol. 2
and study Fig. 12 in that book). If you answered (a) or
(b) read from 'Not all aircraft . . . ' on p. 39 to the end of
the paragraph in Vol. 1 and study Fig. 34.

22   a)   While some aircraft tend to oscillate in the pitching plane
during a spin it should be remembered that the
manoeuvre takes the form of a low speed unbalanced
spiral dive. Therefore the nose must be pitching towards
the centre or axis of the spin i.e. UP in relation to the
pilot. If you answered (b) or (c) read pp. 101–103 in
Vol. 1.

23   c)   During a spin the rolling motion is caused by the yaw so
there is no point in trying to prevent it with aileron,
particularly since the down-going wing will be fully
stalled. The recovery must entail removing the cause of
the spin which is Yaw, and Yaw is controlled with
rudder. If you answered (a) or (b) **as a matter of urgency**
read the whole of Exercise 11 (p. 101, Vol. 1) including
the FLIGHT PRACTICE.

24   a)   Gyroscopic Effect and Asymmetric Blade Effect are only
of consequence when taking-off in a tailwheel aircraft. If
you answered (b) or (c) read DIFFERENCES BETWEEN
NOSEWHEEL AND TAILWHEEL AIRCRAFT p. 109,
Vol. 1 to the end of item 3 (top of p. 110).

25   b)   Using the correct short take-off technique and climbing
at the recommended flaps-down speed, the climb gradient
will improve, although only slightly in the case of most
low-powered light aircraft. However the rate of climb
usually suffers, therefore answer (c) is incorrect. If you
selected answer (a) or (c) read USE OF FLAP DURING
TAKE-OFF pp. 113–114 of Vol. 1 and study Fig. 66.

26   b)   The stalling angle of an airfoil remains the same in level
or banked flight and while answer (c) is partly true it is
misleading because it is the turning force element of the
inclined lift that increases the wing loading. A similar
situation exists when pulling out of a dive or pulling too

tightly around a loop. In each case the wing loading is increased although there is no bank angle. If you answered (a) or (c) read Exercise 15 pp. 146—150 in Vol. 1 and study the illustrations mentioned in the text.

27   b)   Answer (a) refers to Aerodynamic Balance. If you selected (a) or (c) read FLUTTER on p. 22 of Vol. 2 and study Fig. 16.

28   a)   Wash-out is the reduction in angle of incidence towards the wing tip which is built into an aircraft for the purpose of preventing the tendency for a wing to drop at the stall. Frise Ailerons are designed to reduce aileron drag (p. 24 and Fig. 17 in Vol. 2) and Slats have nothing to do with stability (you can read about them under PREVENTING WING DROP AT THE STALL on p. 96 of Vol. 1). If you answered (b) or (c) read LATERAL STABILITY on p. 12 of Vol. 2 and study Figs. 8, 9 and 10.

29   c)   Flutter is caused by a lack of structural rigidity, the penalty of having to reduce airframe weight to a minimum, (see FLUTTER, p. 22 and Fig. 16 in Vol. 2). Aileron Drag has no connection with Horn Balance (read AILERON DRAG, p. 23 and study Fig. 17 in Vol. 2). If you got it wrong read HORN BALANCE, p. 17 in Vol. 2 and study Fig. 11.

30   c)   If you answered (a) or (b) read from 'Conversely it is sometimes . . .' at the top of p. 97 of Vol. 1. to '. . . pre-stall warning buffet.'

31   a)   In effect, lowering an aileron increases the angle of attack and even at low airspeeds this is bound to encourage the full development of a stall. Answer (c) is also incorrect because the up-going aileron is in fact on the wing that has to be lowered during stall recovery. Read THE FULLY DEVELOPED STALL, p. 95 to ' . . . under FLIGHT PRACTICE' on p. 96 in Vol. 1.

32   c)   While it is true that the higher wing loading in a turn will increase the stalling speed this is of little consequence unless the bank angle is steep and 'g' is applied. However

a stall during even a gentle gliding turn is likely to
develop into an incipient spin. If you answered (a) or (b)
read the first paragraph under CLIMBING AND
DESCENDING TURNS on pp. 76–77 of Vol. 1.

33   c)   The Riggers Angle of Incidence is not an angle of attack
and drag could be reduced by flying at a smaller angle
than 3½°–4°. If you answered (a) or (b) read from the
last two lines of p. 6 in Vol. 1 to the end of the first paragraph on p. 8 and study Fig. 12.

34   a)   While the tailplane does compensate for changes in
weight and balance it also compensates for movements of
the centre of pressure, therefore answer (c) is incomplete.
Answer (b) should not be taken too seriously. If you
answered (b) or (c) read THE AEROPLANE, p. 11 to
' . . . of the tailplane clear' on p. 14 of Vol. 1 and study.
Figs. 15, 16, 17, 18, 19 and 20.

35   b)   When one is fitted a faulty nosewheel steering damper
will allow the assembly to vibrate or 'shimmy'. This is not
Wheelbarrowing. If you answered (a) or (c) read
TAKING-OFF, NOSEWHEEL TECHNIQUE, pp. 111–
112 in Vol. 1.

5 Engines and Propellers

Answer		Comments and Study References
1	c)	If you answered (a) or (b) read p. 2, Vol. 4
2	b)	Engine speed is controlled by the Butterfly Valve. If you answered (a) or (c) read p. 3, Vol. 4.
3	a)	The Idle Cut-off has nothing to do with the ignition system. If you answered (b) or (c) read IDLE CUT-OFF p. 26, Vol. 4.
4	a)	It may be called a Four-Stroke Engine but there are two strokes to every revolution (one up and one down). If you answered (b) or (c) read FEEDING THE MIXTURE TO THE ENGINE on p. 3, Vol. 4 and study Fig. 5, p. 14.
5	c)	If you answered (a) or (b) read VALVE MECHANISM, p. 7, Vol. 4 and study Fig. 5, p. 14.
6	b)	(a) is only part of the answer and (c) is wrong. In fact many engines are started on one magneto. If you answered (a) or (c) read DUAL IGNITION on p. 22, Vol. 4.
7	a)	The battery has no connection with magneto ignition and the plug leads are connected to the magnetos all the time. If you answered (b) or (c) read IGNITION SWITCHES on p. 24, Vol. 4.
8	c)	Gravity feed will only work when the tanks are mounted above the engine as in a high-wing monoplane. The throttle-operated accelerator pump would be of little help because it too depends on the carburettor for its supply of fuel. If you answered (a) or (b) read ELECTRIC FUEL PUMP on p. 27 of Vol. 4.

9   a)   Rime, Hoar Frost and Glazed Ice are types of airframe icing. If you answered (b) or (c) read CARBURETTOR ICING, p. 40, Vol. 2 and CARBURETTOR HEAT CONTROL on p. 26, Vol. 4.

10   a)   Severe misfiring is almost invariably due to ignition trouble and sudden power loss will most likely be caused by some form of fuel starvation. If you answered (b) or (c) read CARBURETTOR ICING on p. 40, Vol. 2.

11   b)   Cylinders are made ready for starting either with the primer or the throttle operated accelerator pump. The oil system is self-priming. If you answered (a) or (c) read the last paragraph, p. 26, Vol. 1 and ELECTRIC STARTER on p. 28 of Vol. 4.

12   c)   You fly 'low and slow' for maximum endurance (i.e. maximum time in the air). If you answered (a) or (b) read FLYING FOR RANGE, p. 37, Vol. 2.

13   a)   A competent pilot can keep straight even when the view ahead is reduced by a tail down/nose up attitude. Slipstream, torque and for that matter all four propeller effects act in the same direction. If you answered (b) or (c) read THE TRICYCLE UNDERCARRIAGE, p. 47, Vol. 1, DIFFERENCES BETWEEN NOSEWHEEL AND TAILWHEEL AIRCRAFT, p. 109, Vol. 1 and THE PROPELLER DURING TAKE-OFF, p. 54, Vol. 2.

14   c)   Offset Fin and fixed rudder trim are devices intended to provide feet-off balanced flight at cruising power. Gyroscopic Effect will only occur when the propeller's plane of rotation is altered. If you answered (a) or (b) read p. 51 to '. . . the best arrangement' p. 53 in Vol. 1, also SLIP-STREAM EFFECT and TORQUE EFFECT on p. 55 of Vol. 2.

15   b)   Answer (a) is incorrect because asymmetric blade effect only occurs when the propeller shaft is inclined relative to the aircraft's path along the ground or through the air.

able change in RPM. If you answered (a) or (c) read
ENGINE SPEED INDICATOR, p. 56, Vol. 1, also from
'the propeller's efficiency . . .' p. 46, Vol. 2 to the
bottom of the page. Study Fig. 26.

16 c) A coarse pitch propeller would in fact run at lower rpm,
        thus reducing both noise level and fuel consumption. It
        also prevents the engine developing maximum power for
        take-off. If you answered (a) or (b) read from 'During
        take-off . . . ' on p. 47 of Vol. 2, study Fig. 25 and read
        CONVERSION OF POWER INTO THRUST, p. 19, Vol.
        4.

17 b) Answer (a) is only part of the story and so is answer (c).
        If you selected either of these read PROPELLERS on
        p. 44 of Vol. 2 and study Figs. 25, 26 and 27. Also read
        CONVERSION OF POWER INTO THRUST, p. 19, Vol.
        4.

18 a) A blade failure on any propeller would almost certainly
        cause sufficient vibration to remove the engine from its
        mountings. If you answered (b) or (c) read p. 51, Vol. 2,
        from 'As engines have become. . .'

19 c) Decision Speed (V_1) is the maximum speed on the
        ground that will allow the pilot to abandon the take-off
        and remain on the runway. It does not apply to aircraft
        of less than 12,500 lb maximum weight.
        The figure quoted for V_2 allows a safety margin over
        Minimum Control Speed which is what the term implies.
        If you answered (a) or (b) read FAILURE OF AN
        ENGINE DURING TAKE-OFF on p. 245 of Vol. 2.

20 a) When an engine fails in straight flight or during turns the
        aircraft will always roll towards the dead engine. Since
        roll and yaw are interrelated answer (c) would be quite
        impossible. If you chose (b) or (c) read ENGINE
        FAILURE DURING TURNS, p. 245 in Vol. 2, and study
        Fig. 91.

21 c)   Reducing power during a low-speed turn is bad flying
         technique in any aeroplane and in any case the loss of
         height that will follow such action may present an
         additional danger. Similarly answer (b) involves a height
         loss that may be unacceptable at the time. If you chose
         (a) or (b) read ASYMMETRIC-POWERED MEDIUM
         AND STEEP TURNS on p. 244 of Vol. 2.

22 b)   Why feather the engine when the cause of failure may be
         cured simply by switching on the fuel booster pump? If
         you selected answer (c) read the question again.
         Remember it said there was 'no evidence of serious
         trouble'. If you got it wrong read FAILURE OF AN
         ENGINE DURING CRUISING FLIGHT on p. 241 of
         Vol. 2.

23 a)   When an engine fails yaw is always towards the dead
         engine usually accompanied by a skid towards the live
         engine. If you answered (b) or (c) read INSTRUMENT
         INDICATIONS on p. 244 of Vol. 2.

24 a)   By reducing windmilling drag a feathered propeller may
         in fact lengthen the landing run. Cross-feed may be used
         without having to feather the failed engine, there being
         no connection between the two functions. If you
         answered (b) or (c) read FEATHERING PROPELLERS
         on p. 52 of Vol. 2.

25 a)   Full Throttle Altitude is usually associated with flying for
         maximum range and Thrust is certainly not 'zero' under
         these conditions. If you answered (b) or (c) read
         PRACTISING ASYMMETRIC LANDING AND OVER-
         SHOOT PROCEDURES on p. 252 of Vol. 2.

26 b)   A high outside air temperature has the effect of
         increasing the TAS for any given IAS and the speed
         quoted for V_2 is in any case an IAS. If you answered (a)
         or (c) read OUTSIDE AIR TEMPERATURE, p. 240,
         Vol. 2.

27 c)   Condensation is most likely to occur in the fuel tanks and
         a fuel injection system cannot prevent this. Power output

is not materially affected by choice of induction, i.e.
carburettor or fuel injection. If you answered (a) or (b)
read the paragraph dealing with FUEL INJECTION in the
middle of p. 27 of Vol. 4.

28   c)   In the case of (a) and (b) the most likely result would be
an overspeeding propeller due to excessive fine pitch. If
you gave either of these answers read CONSTANT-
SPEED PROPELLER FAULTS on p. 54 of Vol. 2.

29   b)   The question makes clear that the engine failure has
occurred at the beginning of the climb-out so there may
be insufficient height at that stage to throttle back the
live engine. However by that phase of the take-off and
climb V_2 should have been attained so that a landing
ahead will not be necessary. At any time while in
asymmetric flight aileron may be used to assist rudder.
This is mentioned in the second paragraph on p. 235 and
p. 247 (g), Vol. 2. If you answered (a) or (c) read
ENGINE FAILURE AFTER TAKE-OFF WHEN SAFETY
SPEED HAS BEEN REACHED on p. 248 of Vol. 2.

30   c)   Vents are provided to prevent air locks and fuel strainers
are incorporated for the purpose of detecting water in the
tanks. If you answered (a) or (b) read FUEL SYSTEMS
on p. 82 of Vol. 2.

6 Airframes

Answer		Comments and Study References
1	b)	If you answered (a) or (c) read from 'In 1912 the French . . . ' on p. 31 of Vol. 4 to the end of that section on p. 34. Also study Figs. 11 and 14.
2	a)	Ribs are provided to support the wing skins in an airfoil shape. If you answered (b) or (c) read WING CONSTRUCTION on pp. 34–39 and study Fig. 14 in Vol. 4.
3	c)	Turbulent airflow from the wings may sometimes be felt through the elevators as it moves over the tail surfaces but that is not flutter. Read the first paragraph of AILERONS, ELEVATORS AND RUDDERS, p. 38 to the top of p. 40 in Vol. 4. Also see FLUTTER, p. 22 of Vol. 2 and study Fig. 16 on that page.
4	a)	Static discharge 'wicks' are fitted to some aircraft for the purpose of improving radio reception but these take the form of flexible brushes trailing behind the control surfaces, not small metal tabs. If you answered (b) or (c) read from 'While larger types of aircraft . . . ' on p. 42 of Vol. 4 to the end of the paragraph.
5	c)	Kruger flaps are leading edge devices fitted to some high performance aircraft. If you answered (a) or (b) read FLAPS, pp. 42 and 45 of Vol. 4. Also study Figs. 17 and 18.
6	a)	If you answered (b) or (c) read the first paragraph of UNDERCARRIAGE on p. 47 of Vol. 4.

7   b)   Drum brakes have in fact been operated hydraulically in cars and aircraft for many years and some are of the opinion that they require less maintenance than disc units. If you answered (a) or (c) read BRAKE SYSTEMS on p. 48 of Vol. 4.

8   a)   Brakes powered by the engine or an electro-hydraulic pump are fitted to larger aircraft. If you answered (c) — dear me! Read from 'In light aircraft . . . ', top of p. 50 to the end of that section in Vol. 4 and study Fig. 20.

9   c)   Although there is some merit in answer (b) the prime reason for control locks is explained under TYPES AND PURPOSES OF CONTROL LOCKS on p. 52 of Vol. 4.

10   c)   Answer (a) is incidental to the main function of these struts and (b) is only part of the answer. Read WING CONSTRUCTION on p. 34 in Vol. 4 and look at Fig. 13 on p. 37.

7 Instruments

Answer		Comments and Study References
1	a)	Like the other gyro instruments the turn needle will, if not electrically driven, be powered by a vacuum source. Only the pressure-operated instruments will be affected by a pressure/static blockage. If you answered (b) or (c) read PRESSURE-OPERATED INSTRUMENTS on p. 94 of Vol. 2.
2	b)	For all practical purposes there is no lag in an ASI and Position Error will only affect the accuracy of its readings. If you answered (a) or (c) read ERRORS, p. 95 in Vol. 2.
3	c)	While (a) and (b) are both partly correct they do not individually give the complete answer. If you got it wrong read from the top of p. 95 in Vol. 2.
4	a)	Both height (i.e. reduced atmospheric pressure) and high temperatures for that height will reduce the air density and the greater the reduction the larger the increase in TAS for any RAS. If you answered (b) or (c) study the table at the top of p. 96 in Vol. 2 and try some examples on a computer.
5	a)	Venturi Tubes are more common on older types of air-craft. They are used to supply vacuum to the gyro-operated instruments and there is no connection between the venturi tube and the pressure instruments. If you answered (b) or (c) read THE ALTIMETER on p. 96 of Vol. 2.

6 c) Although the instrument will register height changes of
       20 ft or even less an altimeter is not accurate to these
       limits. If you answered (a) or (b) read ACCURACY on
       p. 100 of Vol. 2.

7 b) If you answered (a) or (c) read BAROMETRIC ERROR
       on p. 98 of Vol. 2.

8 a) The thing to remember here is that high pressure is safe
       and low pressure is unsafe because the aircraft is lower
       than indicated. If you answered (b) or (c) read BARO-
       METRIC ERROR on p. 98 of Vol. 2.

9 c) It would have to be a very steep dive for either (a) or (b)
       to apply. If you chose either of these alternatives read
       LAG ERROR on p. 99 of Vol. 2.

10 b) Since the destination airfield is within the same Altimeter
       Setting Region the QNH already set will apply. On
       landing the altimeter would read 600 ft (the destination
       elevation amsl) at the existing setting. Therefore the
       instrument must be wound down 600 ÷ 30 = 20 mb to
       obtain zero on landing (QFE). If you answered (a) or (c)
       read DETERMINING CIRCUIT HEIGHT AT THE
       DESTINATION AIRFIELD, p. 105 in Vol. 4.

11 b) The bi-metal link or strip will only compensate for
       expansion and contraction of the components within the
       altimeter. It cannot correct changes in the atmosphere
       due to temperature. If you answered (a) or (c) read
       TEMPERATURE ERROR on p. 99 of Vol. 2 and ALTI-
       METER CORRECTIONS on p. 141 of Vol. 4.

12 a) The rather large errors that may be present at quite small
       rates of ascent or descent are the prime reason why the
       VSI should be regarded as an approximate guide to
       vertical change. If you answered (b) or (c) read ERRORS
       on p. 101 to the top of p. 102 in Vol. 2.

13 a) By applying a force towards the centre (from the circum-
       ference) a gyro would simply move in that direction. To
       answer this question you must understand the '90° Rule'.

If you answered (b) or (c) read from 'The second
important property of a gyroscope . . . ' bottom of p. 103
of Vol. 2, and study Fig. 42.

14 b) The Slip Indicator usually takes the form of a damped
pendulum or ball. If you answered (a) or (c) read
PRINCIPLE on p. 106 of Vol. 2, also SLIP INDICATOR
on p. 107.

15 c) Although in some instruments the air supply to the gyro
buckets may discontinue during an extreme attitude
normally these attitudes are only held for a few seconds.
In that time the gyro will continue to spin under its own
momentum. The Pendulous Unit is peculiar to the
Artificial Horizon only and in any case its function is not
to topple the instrument.

16 a) Although the Slip Indicator will give useful information
during a spin recovery it is not a gyro instrument. Only
certain designs of Artificial Horizon have complete
freedom of movement in roll and pitch. Others will have
toppled during the spin and so be unable to assist during
the recovery. If you answered (b) or (c) read THE TURN
AND SLIP INDICATOR on p. 106 to the bottom of
p. 108 in Vol. 2, and study Fig. 44.

17 c) Magnetic Variation is irrelevant because the DI is used to
steer Magnetic Headings, therefore it must be
synchronized with the Magnetic Compass. If you
answered (a) or (b) read FUNCTION on p. 110 of Vol. 2.

18 b) While alternatives (a) and (c) are in themselves correct
they only give part of the answer. Furthermore the
effects of turbulence are a contributing factor of
Mechanical Drift. If you chose (a) or (c) read ERRORS,
MECHANICAL DRIFT and APPARENT DRIFT on
p. 112 and TRANSPORT ERROR, p. 113 of Vol. 2.

19 b) Spring damped gimbals are used in Turn Indicators and
the Pendulous Unit is part of the Artificial Horizon. If
you answered (a) or (c) read APPARENT DRIFT on
p. 112 of Vol. 2.

20   c)   No heading indicator which relies upon a magnetic
          system is suitable for Polar navigation (see Fig. 52 and
          read from 'This fault is called Dip . . .' on p. 83 of Vol. 1
          to the end of that paragraph.) If you answered (a) or (b)
          read HEADING INDICATORS on p. 114 of Vol. 2.

21   a)   While some Artificial Horizons do incorporate a caging
          device that will also erect the gyro not all instruments
          have this and in any case the question asked how the
          function was performed **automatically**. There is a
          counterweight on the horizon bar but its purpose is to
          balance that assembly. If you answered (b) or (c) study
          Figs. 47 and 48 in Vol. 2 and read from 'When toppling
          occurs . . . ' on p. 117 to ' . . . vacuum pump' on p. 119.

22   c)   A climbing turn to the left would be indicated by an
          electrically driven Artificial Horizon where gyro rotation
          is in the opposite direction to vacuum-operated instru-
          ments. If you answered (a) or (b) read ERRORS,
          ACCELERATION and DECELERATION on pp. 119 and
          120 of Vol. 2.

23   b)   The Static Tube or Vent is for the pressure-operated
          instruments (ASI, VSI and Altimeter). If you answered
          (a) or (c) read from 'The gyro . . .' bottom of p. 104 to
          freedom of movement on p. 105 of Vol. 2.

24   c)   While it is true that the magnet system will tilt in relation
          to the horizontal during turns this is caused by the
          normal turning forces and not Dip. Residual Deviation
          after a Compass Swing is called Coefficient A and this
          again has nothing to do with Dip. If you answered (a) or
          (b) read p. 82 of Vol. 1 to '. . . the magnetic compass be-
          comes impracticable', on p. 83. Also study Figs. 52 and 53.

25   b)   While there would be no change in reading while flying
          on a northerly or southerly heading, acceleration and
          deceleration error is most pronounced on east and west.
          If you answered (a) or (c) read from 'On easterly or
          westerly . . . ' to ' . . . return to its true heading'. on p. 84
          of Vol. 1, and study Fig. 55.

26   a)   The thing to note in this question is that it relates to
          flight within the Southern hemisphere, but north or
          south of the Equator the compass will be affected while
          flying wing low unless it is on an easterly or westerly
          heading. If you answered (b) or (c) read from ' under
          certain flight conditions . . . ' on p. 83 to ' . . . Fig. 54
          explains.' on p. 84 of Vol. 1, study Fig. 54 and read the
          fourth paragraph on p. 86.

27   a)   Answer (b) would apply when flying in the southern
          hemisphere and (c) never at all. If you got this wrong
          read from 'To overcome these errors . . . ' at the bottom
          of p. 84 to ' . . . allowed to settle.' on p. 86 of Vol. 1.

28   b)   An out-of-balance indication without turn must be the
          result of crossed controls and reference to the Artificial
          Horizon in this case would confirm that the left wing is
          down. Answer (a) would convert the situation into a left
          turn while (b) would increase the slip to the left. If you
          answered (a) or (c) read STRAIGHT AND LEVEL
          FLIGHT, CLIMBING AND DESCENDING on p. 109 of
          Vol. 2, also item (c) in the Air Exercise on pp. 142 and
          143.

29   b)   If the pressure tube became blocked there would be no
          airspeed indication while the Altimeter and the VSI
          would remain unaffected. Answer (a) means that you
          cannot recognize the difference between a spin and a
          spiral dive; in this case **as a matter of urgency** read THE
          SPIN ON THE LIMITED PANEL on p. 137 of Vol. 2,
          and study Fig. 56.

30   c)   The question makes clear that you are climbing at the
          correct speed, therefore any departure from this, faster
          or slower can only result in a reduction of the existing
          rate of climb. Provided the aircraft is not overloaded or
          flying under 'hot-and-high' conditions an abnormally low
          rate of climb is most likely caused by reduced engine
          power. While there can be many causes of this carburet-
          tor icing is one that is under the control of the pilot.

31   c)   Answer (a) will place the aircraft in a high nose-up
          attitude and this will be followed by a rapid decrease in
          airspeed. While (b) is recommended by some instructors
          it is complex and not very effective due to altimeter lag.
          If you answered (a) or (b) read RECOVERY FROM A
          DIVE on p. 153 of Vol. 2.

32   c)   It is a commonly held but mistaken belief that all Rate 1
          turns, irrespective of IAS are at 15° angle of bank. If you
          answered (a) or (b) read OPERATION IN FLIGHT on
          pp. 121 and 122 of Vol. 2.

33   c)   While answers (a) or (b) could cause the aircraft to turn
          they are not likely to do so suddenly or require
          correcting with a lot of rudder. If you answered (a) or (b)
          read INSTRUMENT FLYING IN MULTI-ENGINED
          AIRCRAFT, p. 139 of Vol. 2.

34   b)   The fact that the aircraft is out of balance when the
          wings are held level must point to incorrect rudder trim.
          In this case it should be adjusted to hold on sufficient
          right rudder to centre the ball. Remember, the ball is
          controlled with rudder. Aileron trim would have been the
          cause had the ball remained in the centre when the wings
          were level. If you answered (a) or (c) read STRAIGHT
          AND LEVEL FLIGHT, CLIMBING AND DESCENDING
          on p. 109 of Vol. 2.

35   b)   Answer (a) is incorrect and incomplete since there is no
          mention of when to stop the turn and (c) will overshoot
          the required heading. If you answered (a) or (c) read
          TURNING on p. 135 of Vol. 2.

8 Radio Aids to Air Navigation

Answer		Comments and Study References
1	c)	A magnetic bearing FROM a station is a QDR. If you answered (a) or (b) read the explanation on p. 57 of Vol. 3.
2	c)	If you answered (a) or (b) read ACCURACY on p. 62 of Vol. 3.
3	a)	All radio transmissions affected by reflection are in varying degrees subject to 'night effect'. If you answered (b) or (c) read from the bottom of p. 58 in Vol. 3 to ' . . . for direction finding purposes (Fig. 21)' on p. 59 and study Fig. 21.
4	b)	If you answered (a) or (c) read the first paragraph under the heading of RADIO MAGNETIC INDICATOR (RMI) on p. 75 of Vol. 3 and study Fig. 25.
5	b)	The question made clear that there was no wind, therefore you can only track on a Heading of 220° when the DI reads 220°. When the NDB is directly behind the aircraft the Radio Compass is bound to read 180°. If you answered (a) or (c) read FLYING OUTBOUND FROM A BEACON on p. 88 of Vol. 3 and study Fig. 33.
6	a)	In questions of this kind always remember that the Radio Compass needle points to the beacon at all times, indicating the progress of the aircraft relative to the transmitter. If you answered (b) or (c) study Fig. 32 on p. 87 of Vol. 3.

7   c)   If you answered (a) or (b) read paragraph 2 on p. 93 of Vol. 3.

8   b)   You cannot fly a holding pattern on an NDB unless you fully understand this question. Therefore if you answered (a) or (c) read HOLDING PATTERNS, pp. 13–16 in Vol. 3, and study Fig. 2.

9   b)   While an EAT is rarely given by the Air Traffic Control Service there are occasions when it becomes necessary and then there must be no misunderstanding the meaning of the term. If you answered (a) or (c) read paragraph 2, p. 94 in Vol. 3.

10 a)   On the basis that the Radio Compass needle always points towards the NDB even when this is behind the aircraft it should not be difficult to determine the direction of drift by imagining the position of the beacon. If you answered (b) or (c) read FLYING OUTBOUND FROM A BEACON, p. 88 of Vol. 3, study Fig. 33 and imagine the effect on the Radio Compass needle should the top aircraft drift to the right. The reading would increase and so reproduce this question.

11 c)   Whether or not the aircraft is working a radio facility of any kind is immaterial. Whenever it is flying above Transition Altitude or Level the Standard Altimeter Setting must be used. If you answered (a) or (b) read ALTIMETER SETTING PROCEDURE on pp. 19–21 in Vol. 3.

12 c)   After an overshoot following an instrument approach there may be high ground/obstructions to avoid and these are noted on let-down charts individually. For safety purposes there is also a minimum safe altitude taking into account these obstructions and this is listed on the chart as 'above sea level' or in other words QNH. An example of this is the note on the Stansted NDB chart illustrated on p. 97 of Vol. 3 where pilots must climb to 2500 ft (QNH) before making another approach.

13   c)   If you answered (a) or (b) read FLYING TO THE
          BEACON on pp. 84—87 in Vol. 3, and study Fig. 32.

14   a)   If you answered (b) or (c) read FLYING OUTBOUND
          FROM A BEACON, pp. 88—89 in Vol. 3, and study Fig.
          33.

15   a)   Answer (b) cannot be correct because a QDR TO is a
          contradiction in terms and so is alternative (c). If you
          selected either of these answers read ORIENTATION
          USING VOR on p. 109 of Vol. 3.

16   c)   If you are drifting to Port the deviation needle will signal
          FLY RIGHT, therefore answer (a) is incorrect. To read
          010° FROM the aircraft would have to be on the other
          side of the VOR beacon. If you answered (a) or (b),
          study Fig. 38 on p. 104 but if you are still in doubt read
          from 'Provided the aircraft . . . ' on p. 102 of Vol. 3 to
          ' . . . away from the VOR' on p. 103.

17   a)   Provided the TO—FROM indicator has been set correctly,
          i.e. showing TO while flying to the VOR beacon and
          FROM when heading away, the deviation needle will
          always give corrective signals. In this case the aircraft has
          approached the beacon with the OBS set on QDM 170°
          TO. On overflying the beacon the instrument will display
          OBS 170° FROM when the deviation needle will
          continue to provide correct 'Fly left/Fly right' infor-
          mation. If you answered (b) or (c) read OMNI-BEARING
          INDICATOR, pp. 100—103, and study Fig. 38 in Vol. 3.
          If the top aircraft were to drift to the left the needle
          would move to the right.

18   c)   If you answered (a) or (b) study Fig. 41 on p. 112 of
          Vol. 3, but imagine that instead of turning on to 090°
          you continue on your present heading of 200°. On
          reaching Radial 270° the deviation needle would swing in
          to the centre, then move away to the left (as seen by the
          pilot). See also Fig. 39 on p. 105.

19 b) Answer (a) would be correct for ILS. If you selected (a)
        or (c) read paragraph 4 of HOMING TO THE BEACON
        on p. 109–110 of Vol. 3.

20 c) When the VOR station is off the air the 'OFF' flag will
        appear but unlike the situation described in this question
        the deviation needle will centre. Nav. receiver failure
        may reproduce various indications depending on the
        nature of the fault but full deflection of the needle with
        the 'OFF' flag showing is unlikely to be one of these. In
        most instruments the TO–FROM indicator is combined
        with the 'OFF' flag (sometimes called the NO SIGNAL
        flag) and when the aircraft departs from the radial set on
        the OBS by 80° or more this will appear until the aircraft
        has flown to within 80° or so of the radial. This is
        mentioned in paragraph 3, p. 111, Vol. 3.

21 b) If you answered (a) or (c) read the note at the start of
        AIR EXERCISE, on p. 109, Vol. 3. When you know the
        accuracy limits in degrees the question may be solved by
        applying the 1-IN-60 Rule.

22 a) A feature of most multi-purpose instruments is that only
        the relevant indications operate when a particular facility
        is selected. For example when a combined VOR/ILS
        indicator is being used on a VOR frequency the
        Glidscope needle will remain inoperative in the central
        position. Likewise when an ILS frequency is selected the
        OBS has no effect on the deviation needle which has now
        become the LOCALIZER needle. If you answered (b) or
        (c) study Fig. 64 on p. 180 in Vol. 3. This shows that the
        OBS and its related Bearing Scale are for VOR purposes
        only.

23 a) If you answered (b) or (c) read FLYING TO AN AIR-
        FIELD on p. 63 of Vol. 3 and study Fig. 23.

24 b) If you answered (a) or (c) read THE SURVEILLANCE
        RADAR APPROACH on p. 169 of Vol. 3.

25 b) If you answered (a) or (c) read THE SURVEILLANCE
        RADAR APPROACH, pp. 169–170, Vol. 3.

26 b) If you answered (a) or (c) read ASSOCIATED AIR-
        BORNE EQUIPMENT, from the bottom of p. 174, Vol.
        3, and study Figs. 61 and 63.

27 c) Unlike VOR there is no TO—FROM indicator in ILS,
        therefore localizer signals (i.e. Fly left—Fly right) are not
        corrective when the aircraft is on a reciprocal heading to
        the runway QDM. While this could be confusing the
        situation is clarified by remembering that the needle
        always indicates left or right of the runway QDM. If you
        answered (a) or (b) read from 'This instrument, which
        forms the . . . ' to the end of the paragraph on p. 176 of
        Vol. 3 and study Fig. 61.

28 a) Since the Glide Path is beamed at a 3° angle backwards
        from the runway threshold it follows that the greater the
        distance from the runway the higher will be the glide
        path. An aircraft approaching the runway at the correct
        height will remain below the Glide Path, usually until
        near the Outer Marker Beacon when the associated
        needle will change from 'Fly-up' to 'Central' indicating
        'On the Glide Path'. If you answered (b) or (c) read from
        No. 6 on p. 188 of Vol. 3 and study Fig. 62 on p. 177.

29 c) If you answered (a) or (b) read ASSOCIATED AIR-
        BORNE EQUIPMENT on pp. 181—183 of Vol. 3, also
        study Figs. 62 and 65.

30 a) Remember that both needles give signals in the corrective
        sense. If you answered (b) or (c), study Figs. 61 and 62.

31 a) Remember that both needles give signals in the corrective
        sense. If you answered (b) or (c) study Figs. 61 and 62.

32 b) The Quadrantal Rule is for the purpose of allowing pilots
        to maintain their own height separation while flying
        outside controlled airspace. If you answered (a) or (c)
        read the paragraph before AIR EXERCISE on p. 193 of
        Vol. 3 and study the pull-out radio-nav. chart (after p.
        196 in Vol. 3). AMBER 25 Airway, running North-South

between Brecon VOR and Wallasey VOR shows EVEN
— running North and — ODD flying South. These refer to
the Flight Levels.

33   c)   If you answered (a) or (b) read FAN MARKERS on p. 82
of Vol. 3, and study Fig. 30.

34   a)   Distance Measuring Equipment means what it says, but
unfortunately, this remarkable aid in basic form can only
measure the distance between the station and the aircraft in a straight line, i.e. air to ground and not ground
position to station. If you answered (b) or (c) read p. 117
and study Fig. 42.

35   c)   Some VHF transmitters are of very high power but even
these rely entirely upon 'Line-of-Sight' reception. In this
respect VHF transmission is rather similar to a light
beam. If you answered (a) or (b) read FREQUENCY
BANDS, pp. 29–32 of Vol. 3, also study Figs. 7, 8 and 9.

9 Airfield Performance, Weight and Balance

Answer		Comments and Study References
1	a)	If you got it wrong read definition 1 on p. 54 of Vol. 4.
2	b)	If you got it wrong read definition 4 on p. 55 of Vol. 4.
3	c)	If you got it wrong read definition 6 on p. 55 of Vol. 4.
4	b)	There is, in fact, a decrease in stability as the C of G moves back. If you answered (a) or (c) read the first two paragraphs on p. 60 of Vol. 4 and study Fig. 21.
5	c)	Centre of Gravity limits relate to maximum foremost and rearmost positions at which the aircraft may balance if stability and control are to remain at a safe level. Position cannot be defined in pound weight or pound-inches. If you answered (a) or (b) read CALCULATING WEIGHT AND BALANCE to the bottom of p. 60 in Vol. 4.
6	a)	The question makes clear that before the weights are added the beam is in balance so answer (b) cannot be correct. If you selected (b) or (c) read METHOD OF COMPUTING BALANCE on p. 62 in Vol. 4, down to '. . . when metric units are used, kg-mm'.
7	b)	Aircraft take-off performance is shown in the performance section of the Owner's/Operating/Flight Manual and you do not need special graphs to determine how much payload is left after fuel has been added (you simply subtract the weight of fuel from the Useful Load; the remainder is payload). If you got it wrong read from 'For small aircraft it is . . . ' on p. 63 of Vol. 4 to the first two lines on p. 66 and look at Fig. 23.

8   c)   To determine whether or not an aircraft is within its
            Centre of Gravity limits both weight and moment must
            be known. These are then related to the Centre of
            Gravity Moment Envelope illustrated on p. 65 (Fig. 25)
            of Vol. 4. If you answered (a) or (b) read the last para-
            graph on p. 66 and study Fig. 24 on p. 64.

9   c)   Be in no doubt about the effect of a tailwind on take-off
            performance. If you answered (a) or (b) read 1 WIND on
            p. 56 of Vol. 4.

10   a)   'Hot and high' airfields provide two conditions that
            contribute to a longer take-off run. If you answered
            (b) or (c) read 3 TEMPERATURE and 4 AIRFIELD
            ELEVATION on pp. 56 and 57 of Vol. 4. Although most
            Owner's/Operating/Flight Manuals give take-off and
            landing performance figures for various airfield elevations
            and temperatures pilots should also understand
            CALCULATING DENSITY ALTITUDE pp. 58 and 59.

11   c)   Not all aircraft exhibit an improvement in take-off
            performance when flap is used. Furthermore rate of
            climb (as opposed to climb gradient) almost invariably
            suffers when flap is selected. If you answered (a) or (b)
            read USE OF FLAP DURING TAKE-OFF, p. 113 of
            Vol. 1 and No. 7 USE OF FLAP on p. 57 of Vol. 4.

12   b)   One would have to be very determined to overload an
            aircraft sufficiently to strain the undercarriage and the
            B/A Ratio is related to spinning, something to avoid in
            multi-engine aircraft. If you answered (a) or (c) read
            BAGGAGE STOWAGE AND MAXIMUM WEIGHT
            ALLOWED to ' . . . an overloaded aeroplane is a
            dangerous one' on p. 59 of Vol. 4.

Index to Flight Briefing for Pilots, Volumes 1–5

Note: Figures in bold type within parentheses indicate volume numbers; Figures in italics indicate the presence of illustrations.